NORHWESTERN
UNIVERSITY
in EVANSTON
ILLINOIS

View from South-West

ANSTON

Lake

CLEVELAND

FORT WAYNE

THE *Centennial*
of NORTHWESTERN UNIVERSITY

A Pictorial History of Northwestern University 1851-1951

Published by

Northwestern University Press

in cooperation with the 1951 Syllabus

EVANSTON   CHICAGO

Foreword

This book is the work of many minds and many hands. Students, alumni and faculty unnamed have contributed sometimes knowingly, sometimes unwittingly, always graciously. The writing was done largely by John M. Norris, graduate assistant in history, based to a great extent upon a much longer manuscript prepared by Dean James Alton James. Dr. James has worked assiduously to make both condensation and new material accurate in detail. The pictures (for which acknowledgements will be found at the end of the volume) were discovered, sorted and arranged by Rollin S. Thompson assisted by Prof. Floyd Arpan and many others. A special word of thanks must go to Miss Florence Stewart of the University Archives, who has helped at every turn. Edward Stromberg and his office have been most cooperative. But space is lacking to give each one his due. Representatives from all the schools of the University have participated, and all of the committee members named below have given of their time and their talents.

Cooperation by the *Syllabus* staff and the Students Publishing Co. on the one hand and the University committee of alumni and faculty on the other have made possible various features which otherwise would have been lacking.

This is not a complete history—of that we are keenly aware. It is a sampling. It can not describe the years of devoted service of people like Ruth Jackson in the library, it can not picture every fraternity house or even mention every dean. The memory or the imagination of each reader will call to mind many another inspiring teacher, many a generous donor, many a football great, though other names are here chosen as examples. This book can not rival in completeness either the catalogs or the *University Register*.

What the *Pictorial History* does attempt to do is to epitomize the history of the University as a whole, not of the separate Schools. The trivial and the momentous are deliberately blended, for so they are in university life everywhere. Hence this volume is a review, however imperfect, of the complex panorama which has unfolded on the shores of Lake Michigan through the past one hundred years.

This kaleidoscope of the past does not imply a completed development. The century that is gone is merely a prelude to the opportunities and achievements which the coming centuries will bring.

Our hope is that the alumnus may have here some moments of pleasant memories, that the friend of the University may gain a new sense of acquaintanceship, that the prospective student may feel something of the traditions and the character of the institution, that all may understand a bit more fully the people and the organizations and the ideals which have made Northwestern in the past, and with which she looks to the future.

F.D.S.

Editorial Staff

The Centennial Committee on the Pictorial History

Barry J. Anson,
Professor of Anatomy

Floyd G. Arpan,
Associate professor of Journalism

Edward L. Clark,
Associate professor of Psychology

Mrs. Edson B. Fowler,
Arts '92, former Trustee

Rollin S. Thompson, *Editor of the 1951 Syllabus*
Picture Editor

Franklin D. Scott, *Professor of History*
Chairman
Editor

CONSULTANT

James Alton James, *Dean of the Graduate School, Emeritus*

EX OFFICIO

Edward H. Stromberg, *Director of Publicity and Publications*
Albert C. Van Dusen, *Assistant to the President for the Centennial*

Assistants from the Syllabus

Peter Jacobi, *Research*

Rosemarie Knuti, *Captions*
Sue Taub, *Art*

Marianne Christy, *Engraving*
Barbara Kandelman, *Printing*

Table of Contents

CANADA

MINNESOTA

Lake Superior

DULUTH

MICH

WISCONSIN

NEAPOLIS
ST. PAUL'

OSHKOSH

Lake Michigan

Lake Huron

MADISON

NORTHWESTERN · UNIVERSITY
1851
1951

EVANSTON
AND
CHICAGO

EAST
LANSING

DETROIT

ANN ARBOR

Lake Erie

LOUISIANA PURCHASE

CLEVELAND

FORT WAYNE

OHIO

PEORIA

BLOOMINGTON

CHAMPAIGN

SPRINGFIELD

URBANA

LA FAYETTE

COLUMBUS

INDIANAPOLIS

CINCINNATI

BLOOMINGTON

N

EVANSVILLE

A MAP OF THE

S

CAIRO

Northwest Territory

*as established by the
Ordinance of 1787, showing the
Location of Northwestern University*

THE BEGINNINGS
1851-1890

THE BEGINNINGS

1851~1890

John Evans

Grant Goodrich

Orrington Lunt

I T was a year of uncertainty. North and South had become more than geographic terms. President Zachary Taylor puzzled over the slavery problem while Henry Clay wrote a Compromise to preserve the Union. In the West, Manifest Destiny and gold made California a state, and the Latin neighbors of the Republic watched apprehensively as the frontier pushed west and south.

In Illinois, too, the pace was quickening. Stephen A. Douglas was already a familiar name and an ex-Congressman from Springfield named Abraham Lincoln was riding the court circuit in the southern part of the state. Along the shore of Lake Michigan the booming city of Chicago, just seventeen years old, already counted almost thirty thousand people, but scoffed at the fantastic prediction of one of her citizens that she would reach 200,000 within a generation. Mud, plank roads, and land speculation, lake traffic, the grain trade and Cyrus McCormick's reaper were things of daily concern. People seeking culture turned from the materialism of 1850 to the "higher things" and attended "Professor" O. S. Fowler's lectures on phrenology at the City Hall, or borrowed books from the wonderful new thousand-volume library of the Lyceum. The City Fathers struggled with the problems of lack of sewers, recurrent epidemics, grog shops, and the prevalence of pickpockets. Citizens pointed with pride

WITH THE UNIVERSITY CHARTER featured in the center are some of Northwestern's historical landmarks. Clockwise starting at upper left are Chicago Medical College, Hall of Science, Women's College, Preparatory School, Life Saving Station, Snyder farm house, and University Hall tower.

11

1853—AERIAL OF CHICAGO, twenty years old, boasting a rapidly growing population of over 30,000.

to the new $75,000 Tremont House at the corner of Lake and Dearborn Streets, and duly resented the description by a "down-Easter" of Chicago as "of all the prairie towns, the most repulsive to every human sense."

To the north, along the lakeshore, and west of the swamp that ran between the present Chicago and Ridge Avenues, lay the township of Ridgeville. Here lived some 443 persons, among them some outcasts and ne'er-do-wells from Chicago. Communication with Chicago was along the Green Bay Road which wound its way through swamps and oak forests toward Milwaukee. The civic and social center of the community was the Buckeye Tavern.

Founding the University, 1850-1855

On the last day of May, 1850, nine friends met in the office of Grant Goodrich, on Lake Street in Chicago. After a prayer they set themselves to consider the establishment of a university for the Northwest, "under the patronage of the Methodist Episcopal Church." The need for a university in the Northwest was certainly apparent. The Ordinance of 1787 had declared that: "Religion,

12

morality and knowledge being necessary to good government and the happiness of mankind, schools and the means of education shall be forever encouraged." Nevertheless higher education in Illinois in 1850 was represented almost solely by a few denominational colleges far downstate. Such institutions as "Professor" Hathaway's Academy, which offered to teach "any part of a collegiate course desired," were hardly to be considered.

That the Methodist Church took the initiative in improving this situation was, in part, an indication that the great intellectual development of American Methodism, which had begun with Francis Asbury and Thomas Coke, was in full tide. The General Conference of 1820 had proposed the establishment of schools and colleges and the General Conference of 1848 determined that their nature should be liberal, neither "Godless" nor narrowly sectarian. In addition to a strong belief in the future of Chicago, denominational pride was a major factor in determining the establishment of Northwestern. Matthew Simpson, distinguished Methodist clergyman of Indiana and, with Dr. John Evans, one of the originators of the idea of the University, expressed this denomi-

national concern in his statement: "If there is a single point on which the public regard us unfavorably, it is the matter of education. They acknowledge our piety, they know our numbers, they admit our energy and enterprise, but they have not given us credit for being deeply interested in education."

The meeting of the nine in Chicago on May 31, 1850, passed a single resolution, to appoint a committee of five to draft a charter to be submitted to the legislature and to notify the Rock River and neighboring conferences of the Methodist Church of the proposed plan, asking their support. Another committee of three was appointed to find the money for the new institution. The University, in the liberal tradition of Methodism, was to be broadly inclusive as to religious policy. Perhaps its most important characteristic, however, was that it was designed to serve the whole Northwest Territory. Of the twenty-eight colleges in the Middle West chartered prior to 1850, twenty-three denominational and five under state control, none claimed to serve anything more than local needs. It was the hope of the founders that Northwestern University would, in the Middle West, achieve the same position as a great center of higher learning as that held in the Old World by Oxford, the birthplace of Methodism.

Dr. John Evans, the most remarkable of this very remarkable group of young men, was made chairman of the finance committee. He was "a dreamer of great dreams, with ability and force of character to make them come true." In his varied occupations then and later, of pioneer physician, founder of hospitals, real estate promoter, builder of railroads and Lincoln's war governor of Colorado territory, he combined a high degree of determination, courage and business acumen with a strong and practical Christian faith. Historical evidence supports the fact that Dr. Evans was the originator, inspired by Matthew Simpson, of the idea of Northwestern University and for more than forty years he was the chief support of the University, devoting time, money and energy in large quantities to secure the successful foundation and survival of this, his most important achievement.

The remaining eight founders of the Uni-

RIDGEVILLE'S BUCKEYE TAVERN served town patrons and welcomed travelers on Green Bay Trail.

1840—LOG HOUSE, built by Carl Eiseman on Niles Road, was a picturesque landmark of early days.

1847—McCORMICK REAPER FACTORY, symbolizing Chicago's beginnings of industry, is typical of businesses that have aided growth of Northwestern.

versity were little less remarkable than Dr. Evans. They included three lawyers, Grant Goodrich, Henry W. Clark and Andrew J. Brown; two business men, Orrington Lunt and Jabez Botsford; and three Chicago Methodist ministers, Richard Haney, Richard A. Blanchard and Zadoc Hall. Not one of these men had attended a college although some of them had been students at seminaries and Dr. Evans was a graduate of Lynn Medical College, Cincinnati.

Grant Goodrich was one of the first lawyers in Chicago, coming to the community in 1834.

His career as a civic official, judge and prominent Methodist layman mirrored the progress of Chicago during its first half century of existence. Significant of his time and religious background were Mr. Goodrich's support for the anti-slavery movement and his interest in promoting higher education in the Middle West.

Orrington Lunt, another of the more influential founders, like many of the early patrons and administrators of Northwestern, was a native of New England. In Chicago he became a prominent grain trader and land promoter. For more than thirty years, in cooperation with Dr. Evans, who became his brother-in-law, he upheld the University in all the many crises of its fortunes and his name is among the most honored in the history of Northwestern.

The University's legal existence was assured on January 28, 1851, when the charter became law. By its provisions the trustees, thirty-two in number, were to be responsible for the administration of the University's business affairs, for organizing a faculty and curriculum, for making by-laws and for grant-

DEMPSTER HALL, former quarters of Garrett Biblical Institute, was acquired as men's dormitory for University in late 1860's. Channel of the Rubicon, a stream cutting campus during the early days, is in foreground.

HUNTOON HOUSE was first frame structure in Evanston. For many years it served as city's Old Post Office.

ing degrees. Dr. Evans was elected president of the board of trustees and an executive committee began the work of giving the University a faculty and a curriculum.

Dr. Clark Titus Hinman, principal of Wesleyan Seminary (now Albion College, Michigan), and one of the representatives of the Michigan Methodist Conference on Northwestern's board of trustees, was elected president of the University in 1853. He was a young man of great force of character and was able to persuade the trustees to adopt a plan for the University which was far more elaborate than anything they had envisaged. Hinman desired a university for the whole Northwest, endowed with at least $500,000, made up of several schools and colleges and equal in its standards to the best universities in the East. The plan was adopted in part, with the setting up of an easily expansible College of Literature, Science and the Arts, consisting of fourteen departments.

This ideal of a real university remained,

OLD COLLEGE, University's first building, as it looked in 1855 when it welcomed first students. It stood then at northwest corner of Davis street and Hinman avenue.

FINANCIAL PROBLEMS of University were great in early days. To reduce them, perpetual scholarships were sold at $100, giving free tuition to donor's descendents.

with some lapses, the goal of succeeding administrations. Hinman, however, lived only to see the preliminaries under way, for he became the first martyr in his own cause. During the eighteen months of his presidency, Dr. Hinman attempted to achieve the financial goal of $250,000 endowment, through the sale of scholarships. He did, in fact, receive pledges totaling $60,000 but his tremendous efforts in this cause affected his health and after a short illness he died in October, 1854. It was a great blow to the University, since his influence had attracted the promise of much financial support, some of which was not forthcoming after his death.

15

By 1853, the University had a president, a curriculum and two professors—Henry S. Noyes and William D. Godman. Its financial resources, while not approaching Dr. Hinman's proposed mark, were sufficient to enable the new institution to plan for its opening. It was now time to find a site and build some tangible proof of the University's existence. A committee, including Lunt and Evans, had been searching for a site for the past year. Dr. Hinman had persuaded the trustees not to build the University in Chicago, and various suburban locations, among them Jefferson, near the present Oak Park, were considered. One August day in 1853, however, Orrington Lunt went for a drive with a friend

Philo Judson, the University's business agent. A community, named Evanston in 1854, was planned to sustain the University, and civilization marched in from Chicago almost overnight. Streets were laid out and a hotel was built. The University practiced far-sighted generosity in its donation of land to the city for parks and public schools and to churches for building sites. A community church was organized and grog shops were invited to leave town by an amendment to the University charter in 1855, which forbade the sale of liquor within four miles of the University campus. Simultaneously another amendment provided that all University property, up to the extent of 2,000 acres,

Clark Titus Hinman
President
1853 - 1854

Philo Judson
Business Manager
1853 - 1887

along the North Shore. The high sandy bluffs and oak forests along the lake east of Ridgeville fascinated him, and he persuaded the trustees to come out and see them. "We were delighted—some of the brethren threw up their hats. We had found the place." Three hundred seventy-nine acres were purchased for $25,000. The purchase was made by Dr. John Evans, who personally paid $1,000 in cash and became responsible for a mortgage on the balance. This price represented a 5,000 per cent profit for Dr. John Foster, the reluctant seller.

Nevertheless the purchase of the land proved a profitable investment for the University. Some of it was sold in lots at a three hundred per cent advance on cost price by

could be held forever tax-free. The Chicago and Milwaukee Railroad came to town from Chicago in 1854 and land values rose. Drinking water had to be taken from the lake and the butcher called twice a week from Chicago as Evanston passed through its boom town stage into quiet respectability.

The revenue of the University increased steadily with the development of Evanston. The property at the corner of La Salle and Jackson Streets in Chicago, which was purchased in 1851 as a possible site for a preparatory school, was held for investment purposes on the insistence of Dr. Evans, and today is one of the most profitable investments of the University. On the initiative of Dr. Evans a similar policy of leasing was adopted

MANY FAMOUS TRAVELERS stopped at passenger station of Chicago, Milwaukee, and St. Paul railway.

with most of the Evanston holdings. Sale of land, leases, and solicitation and sale of scholarships made possible a favorable balance on paper of over $50,000 in the University's accounts in 1854, enough to erect a building and begin teaching.

Struggle of the College, 1855-1869

On June 15, 1855, the University really began its existence when the cornerstone of Old College at the northwest corner of Davis Street and Hinman Avenue was laid with much ceremony. The building was opened on November fifth in the presence of the faculty of two (Professor Henry S. Noyes acting as President), trustees, townspeople and the four students. The press described the structure as "a superb building of three stories having ten large airy rooms besides the chapel." Although Old College has since served as a college, preparatory school and School of Education, and has undergone two transplantings, it still retains something of the atmosphere of 1855. It may be of interest to record that the early trustees of 1855 considered Old College as merely a temporary structure and not, as has sometimes been rumored, as a perpetual monument to the founding of the University.

FIRST METHODIST CHURCH, north shore landmark built in 1856, was Evanston's first house of worship.

Henry Sanborn Noyes
Acting President
1854 - 1856

PROGRAM OF 1865 DEBATE between Hinman and Adelphic literary societies. Exciting topics include "Spartacus to the Gladiators" and "On Being Found Guilty of High Treason."

Randolph Sinks Foster
President
1856 - 1860

North-Western University.

Prize Declamation

OF THE

HINMAN & ADELPHIC SOCIETIES,

Evanston, June 30th, 1865, at 8 P. M.

PROGRAMME.

Prayer.

1. On being found Guilty of High Treason, - - EMMETT.
R. W. CROSS.

2. Spartacus to the Gladiators, - - - - - - KELLOGG.
C. K. OFFIELD.

3. The four Master Spirits of the World,
C. C. SNYDER.

4. The Death Penalty, - - - - - - - - - - HUGO.
W. C. COMSTOCK.

Music.

5. Irish Aliens, - - - - - - - - - - - - SHEIL.
S. B. RAYMOND.

6. The Diver,
J. COPELAND.

7. Spartacus to the Roman Envoys,
T. R. STROBRIDGE.

8. Patriotic Speech, - - - - - - - - DICKINSON.
R. D. SHEPARD.

Benediction.

The first college year was uncertain and precarious. Classes were conducted in the classical, elective and scientific departments. One thousand dollars, appropriated for a library, was allocated to the natural science department. The year was divided into three terms of thirteen weeks each and public examinations were held at the close of each term, and at the end of the sophomore and senior years. Entrance requirements for all three departments included a rigorous drill in the classics and higher mathematics. It was soon discovered, however, that "the majority of young men within the limits of our patronage are not prepared for the college course." It was not until a preparatory department was definitely established in 1859 that this handicap was overcome.

Another disadvantage to the University was the fact that most of the first class attended on scholarships. As the tuition was $45.00 a year, the revenue of the University from fees was only $175.00 for the first year, of which $71.75 was paid to the janitor. Disbursements were on a similarly modest scale, since the faculty had only two members. Pro-

fessor Henry S. Noyes, in customary Prince Albert and silk hat, fulfilled the functions of acting president, professor of mathematics, acting professor of moral philosophy and rhetoric, treasurer, and teacher of the Sunday Bible class. Professor William D. Godman, similarly garbed, was professor of Greek, acting professor of Latin, secretary, and librarian in charge of "1,917 volumes, 21 catalogues and 16 pamphlets."

In 1856 Dr. Randolph Sinks Foster, a prominent Methodist clergyman of New York City, was invited to fill the vacancy left by the death of President Hinman. After stipulating a year's leave of absence, he accepted. As a scholar and clergyman, no less than in his understanding of and sympathy with youth, Foster was suitable for the post. He set and maintained high standards of teaching, and was a leader in what little social activity there was on the campus. His chief drawback in the eyes of the trustees was his complete inability in money matters, but fortunately these could be left to Philo Judson and Professor Noyes.

In 1856 the Trustees were informed by

"D. Bonbright" that, "I have the honor to receive your communication informing me of my election to the professorship of Latin in Northwestern University. I have the pleasure hereby to signify my acceptance of election." In accepting the invitation, Professor Bonbright stipulated that he should be free for one year to continue his professional preparation in Europe. He studied for two years at Berlin, Göttingen and Bonn, establishing even in that early day Northwestern's tradition of extensive post graduate preparation for its faculty members. In 1858 Bonbright began his teaching of the classics which was for fifty-four years one of the principal elements contributing to the success of the Liberal Arts curriculum. He lived in the memory of one student as "standing there with his hands beneath his coat-tails, with his eyes fixed on the cob-webs in the cornice, and in his rich bass voice repeating the Odes of Horace. As he spoke we could see the Gods upon Olympus and the snow-white mountain top of Soracte."

Regulation of student conduct during these early years was necessarily strict. Gambling, drinking or habitual disorderliness incurred a punishment of dismissal, while absences from prayers, recitations or Sunday religious services as well as the students' academic standing were recorded for presentation to anxious parents on request. Parents were urged to deposit funds for students' use with faculty members, who could oversee their expenditure. The University circulars could claim with some justification that: "We have never seen a community anywhere in which so large a preponderance of opinion was strictly moral and religious. Parents may send their sons here with the utmost confidence that they will be placed at a distance from temptation."

There is almost no record of extracurricular student life during these early years. The small numbers (registration had reached only 36 by the fourth year) should have made close association of students easy, but this was counterbalanced by the fact that all but four of the students were boarded with families in the town. The Hinman Literary Society, founded in 1855 and named in memory of the first president, was the first attempt at extracurricular organization. It met in the afternoons (to save candle-light), heard papers by the faculty or seriously debated such questions as: "Resolved, that the Pilgrim Fathers were justified in their treatment of the North American Indian," or, of more current interest: "That literal translations of the Greek

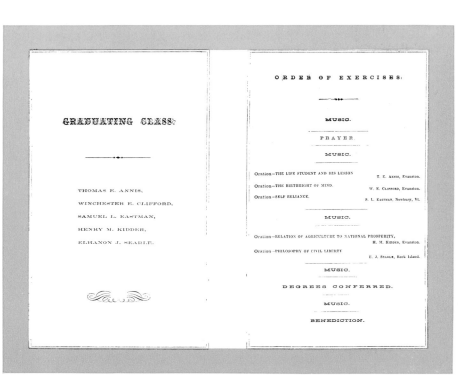

ONLY FOUR OF TEN original freshmen and one student who entered later held on long enough to graduate at Northwestern's first commencement in June, 1859.

FIRST BUILDING of Northwestern Female College. School was independently founded by William Jones, in 1855.

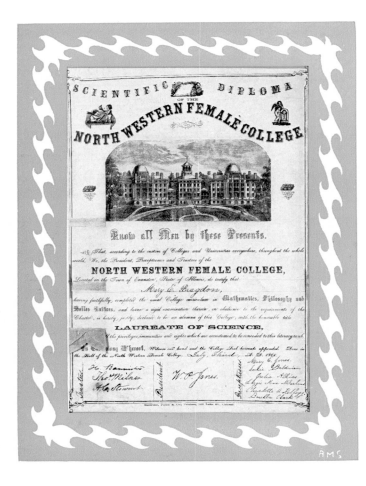

OPPOSITION BY Northwestern men who believed women belonged in the home did not deter brave ladies of Northwestern Female College, who received diplomas such as this for completing their course.

and Latin classics are injurious to college students using them in connection with their course of studies."

Faculty families showed a kindly concern for the social life of the students, and organized parties and church "sociables," in which the students of the Northwestern Female College participated. Unsophisticated fun was the chief feature of these gatherings, although one student from nearby Garrett Biblical Institute pursued a young lady of the Female College with the thought-provoking theological conundrum: "What, in your judgment, is the dividing line that separates sin from holiness?"

Cultural influences were expanding in Frances Willard's "Classic Town," and now Evanston had a college for young ladies and a theological seminary. In 1855 William P. Jones began the Northwestern Female College. Its beginnings were inauspicious, since in addition to entrenched male prejudice against higher education for women, the Female College had to struggle with a continual shortage of funds and the early destruction of its first building by fire. The College's academic standards were high for such a pioneer institution, comparable, in fact, to those of the University. The disciplinary regulations were also rigorous, as one junior recorded: "Heard the rules and regulations of

A $10 DONATION TO GARRETT entitled donor to copy of this picture of Mrs. Garrett, early benefactress.

the school—a good many to be sure, but I guess we shall be able to keep them."

The relations of the College with the University were stormy. The trustees of the University, already distrustful of such an institution as a college for women, were naturally annoyed when the name "Northwestern" was usurped. Furthermore, the problem of discipline among the University students was increased by the proximity of the two institutions. Professor Jones certainly agreed with the trustees on this last point. His life was embittered with foiling attempts of students of both institutions to thwart the rather rigid demands of nineteenth century propriety. It proved impossible to prevent occasional unchaperoned moonlight walks, going to church in couples and other such offenses. On the other hand, attempts by the ladies to invade male spheres of activity, such as debating and essay-writing, caused considerable resentment on the part of the men, although they invited the girls to attend the debates of the Hinman Society when the subject of debate was: "The Rights of Women to the Suffrage."

It was more than a decade before the union of the two institutions was achieved, and the steps by which this was accomplished were many and complicated. In 1869 the board of trustees of the University voted to admit women to the University. In the same year Professor Jones retired and the facilities of the Northwestern Female College were taken over by the Ladies' Educational Association which founded the Evanston College for Ladies in its place. A new building, the present home of the School of Music, was begun in 1871, but the Chicago Fire of that year delayed its construction and made unification with the University more than ever necessary. It was not until 1873, however, that, after long negotiation, the Evanston College for Ladies became at last the Women's College of Northwestern University, and Frances Willard, its former president, became Northwestern's first dean of women.

Across the "Rubicon" ditch on the north campus, Garrett Biblical Institute was rapidly developing as the Methodist seminary of the Middle West under the presidency of Dr. John Dempster. It was named for the shrewd and colorful Chicago auctioneer, Augustus Garrett, and was financed by his pious wife, Eliza. In 1855 the first frame structure, Dempster Hall, was built on land donated by the University. By the terms of its charter the Institute was to remain forever independent, but a few of the same men served on both boards of trustees and the association

GARRETT ROUND HOUSE, built of driftwood found by students, served as dormitory in early Garrett days.

LATE 1860'S were years of expansion. Heck Hall was built in 1867. University Hall was completed in 1869.

between the two institutions has always been very close.

The year 1857 was an eventful one for the University. President Foster was inaugurated and James G. Blaney became Professor of Natural Science. Talented Robert Kennicott, later founder of the Chicago Academy of Arts and Sciences, began the Museum on the third floor of Old College, and was a founder of scientific research in the University. The Hinman Society debated the respective merits of Lincoln and Douglas as political leaders of Illinois.

Such matters were pushed into the background, however, when the expanding frontier overreached itself and the Panic of 1857 cast its long shadow over the University. In an atmosphere of lagging business, tightened credit and threatened bankruptcy, Northwestern's trustees instituted a regime of rigid economy. Faculty salaries went into

arrears and even the more pressing expenditures were cancelled. Despite these measures there was a deficit of $3,000 on an expenditure of $5,000 in 1858, and faculty members were asked to take part of their arrears of salary in unproductive University real estate. Meanwhile, the trustees were soliciting contributions for a new permanent building in order to restore confidence in the future of the University. Donors of $1,000 or more were to have fellowships named for them and those who contributed $5,000 or more could endow a chair. Despite these inducements, however, the trustees failed to achieve their goal of $30,000 and the subscriptions lapsed. It was only gradually that the University recovered from the setbacks of this year.

In June of 1859 the long-awaited first commencement was held. After the ordeal of three days of public examination, four survivors of the original class of ten freshmen were awarded the degree of Bachelor of Arts, and one later entrant the degree of Bachelor of Philosophy. An address was delivered by Dr. Evans in which the past of the University was proudly reviewed and its future confidently predicted. In the course of his remarks Dr. Evans appeased the dissatisfaction of persons whose sons had not been admitted to preparatory instruction on scholarships. The difficulty was removed and he hoped that "the self-sacrificing and laborious gentlemen of the faculty would be sustained in this and the preparatory department crowded."

Slowly the University recovered from the damage of 1857. Seven students were graduated in the class of 1860 and an enrollment of 600 was predicted for the near future. Dr. Foster left to take up a pastorate in New York, and after the refusal of Dr. Erastus O. Haven, editor of the Methodist weekly *Zion's Herald* and former Professor of History and English Literature at the University of Michigan, to take his place, Professor Noyes again became Acting President.

One September night in 1860 the steamer *Lady Elgin* sank off Winnetka. Next morning the full horror of the situation was revealed to the helpless watchers lining the shore, as Edward Spencer, a student who was also an

HOUSE ON THE SNYDER FARM, which the University purchased for land, was an early Ridgeville home.

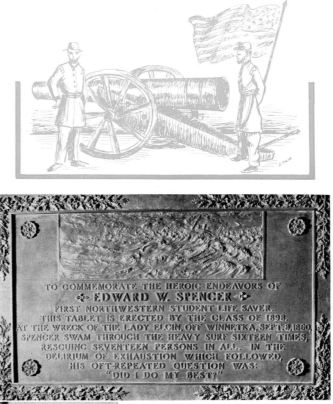

IN 1898 the University dedicated this plaque to Edward Spencer, who saved seventeen from drowning in the Lady Elgin disaster.

LADY ELGIN, excursion steamer, collided on Lake Michigan with schooner Augusta on September 8, 1860, during storm. The tragedy occurred two days after this picture was made.

23

1856—FIRST UNIVERSITY LIBRARY was started on a $3,000 fund voted by the Board of Trustees. Space was provided in University Hall after 1869 for study and storage of books. Cast iron stove provided localized heat.

expert swimmer, rescued seventeen survivors from the pounding surf and Northwestern acquired its first hero. It almost acquired a life-saving station as well, for public opinion demanded the construction of a station, but the War between the States prevented immediate action, and eleven years passed by before the demand was answered.

That autumn there were many important things to think about. The Hinman Society and the newly-formed Adelphic Society debated the significance of Harper's Ferry, and Mr. Lincoln, fresh from Cooper Union, visited his friend Julius White of Evanston, and was serenaded by the students. South Carolina seceded and the new President of the United States expressed the hope in his First Inaugural that: "The mystic chords of memory . . . will yet swell the chorus of the Union, when again touched, as they surely will be, by the better angels of our nature."

Soon he was making another appeal, for twenty-five thousand volunteers, because Fort

Sumter had fallen and war had begun. Allen W. Gray of the University class of '63 marched away to Chickamauga, Mission Ridge and Kenesaw Mountain (coming back for his degree in 1912), and William H. Raleigh of Maryland took the long Southern road that led to Appomattox. A rush of volunteers to the colors was temporarily delayed by the Sunday closing of the Chicago recruiting office, but soon John A. Page was on his way to Cairo and "Drill! drill! drill! . . . Articles of war or regulations were a myth to us. We were obedient, and performed our allotted tasks because we had been brought up to do so. We did not have any reverence for rank, nor did we appreciate the difference between a general, colonel or captain."

On the home front, the girls of the Female College prepared hospital supplies and mended an old flag, to fly at the masthead for the inspiration of the whole town. The more belligerent men organized the Union League to defeat Copperhead machinations, and

Bishop Simpson's condemnation of the Confederacy lived in Frances Willard's memory, as an occasion when "the very air seemed surcharged with the thunder and lightning of God's wrath against secession and slavery."

The exciting novelty of the war disappeared as the casualty returns came in and the Evanston Company of the Eighth Cavalry charged at Gettysburg. Alphonso Linn, a tutor of Latin, raised a platoon of University Guards and marched away to die of typhoid fever at Cairo. Professor Blaney resigned his professorship to enter the army. Then the firing ceased in 1865 and the University counted the cost. Seventy-seven Northwesterners, colonels, majors, captains, chaplains, doctors, sergeants and privates, had gone to the war and seven were dead.

Despite the decline in the student body caused by the call to the colors, the revenue of the University increased rapidly from the war appreciation of its property. The indebtedness of the 1850's was liquidated by 1868 and more land was purchased on the North Shore, including the Snyder Farm south of Dempster Street in Evanston. Nor

OLD UNIVERSITY MUSEUM, pride of the University in the 1860's, filled with fossils, skeletons and students.

FIRST CAMPUS EXTRA CURRICULAR activity was Hinman Literary Society founded in 1855 for "mutual improvement in mind, manners, and fraternal regards." Group met in later years in University Hall, among appropriate decorations and furniture.

was the expansion of the University itself neglected. A gesture toward the beginning of graduate work was made when degrees of Master of Arts and Master of Philosophy were first awarded in 1863. Scholarships were instituted for Chicago high school graduates, and the Preparatory School was given a permanent status.

The Museum was expanded and enlarged by Dr. Oliver Marcy, Dr. Blaney's successor as professor of natural science. Dr. Marcy was one of the most distinguished naturalists in the country, being an authority on the geology of the Northwest and having served as naturalist on the federal government's road survey through Idaho and Montana in 1865. For thirty-seven years this beloved teacher served as professor of natural history and physics and at various times added to his duties those of teacher of zoology, moral science, philosophy, natural theology, mathematics, geology, mineralogy, botany, chemistry, physiology, logic and Greek, in addition

David Hilton Wheeler
Acting President
1867 - 1869

Erastus Otis Haven
President
1869 - 1872

Charles Henry Fowler
President
1872 - 1876

to being twice acting president of the University.

Expansion and Affiliation, 1869-1881

The new prosperity of the University was reflected in the opening, in 1869, of the first permanent building, University Hall. The successful completion of this "elegant and commodious structure" owed much to the architectural talents of Professor Bonbright and even more to the financial ability of Professor Noyes. With its chemical laboratory, library, chapel, dormitories and museum, the University now felt better equipped for its task. Heck Hall, a dormitory building for the theological students donated by the Methodist women's organizations, had just been completed on the present site of Deering Library. The final campus plan was made as a result of these new additions and Dempster Hall, the former quarters of the Biblical Institute, was acquired as a men's dormitory for the University.

The year 1869 also saw the addition of a medical school to the University. In 1857 Dr. Nathan Smith Davis, having failed to persuade his colleagues at Rush Medical College to institute certain improvements in the curriculum, with Drs. H. A. Johnson and Edmund Andrews, transferred his ideas and leadership to the newly-chartered Lind University in Chicago. His stated purpose was "to put into practical operation a system of medical college instruction more in accordance with sound educational principles and better adapted to the present state of the science or art of medicine, than that which has been so long adhered to by the medical schools of the country."

Four floors of the Lind block and the clinical facilities of Mercy Hospital were secured and a medical museum and free dispensary were established. In 1863 the school had become independent as Chicago Medical College when

1874—NORTHWESTERN CAMPUS from Evanston Municipal Pier. Lake steamers unloaded passengers and cargo here until railroad era developed. Panoramic sweep discloses University Hall, Old College, Heck Hall, and light house.

1857—LIND UNIVERSITY in Chicago opened its medical school in this building on South Dearborn street.

1863—LIND COLLAPSED and its medical school became Chicago Medical College, located on Prairie avenue.

Lind University collapsed with the bankruptcy of its benefactor. Six years later it became the Medical Department of Northwestern University, with Dr. Davis as dean. The University gave $15,000 for a new building, endowed a chair of chemistry and agreed to grant the degree of M.D. only on the recommendation of the Chicago Medical College. Apart from these provisions, the Chicago Medical College retained its name and full control of its own affairs until 1891.

Professor Noyes was no longer in charge of the University when these improvements were completed. The strain of holding the University together during the war years had broken his health and he retired in 1867, dying in 1872. Professor David H. Wheeler succeeded him as acting president but his administration lasted only two years, for the trustees had finally determined to appoint a permanent president. Dr. Erastus O. Haven, their choice, was perhaps the most brilliant of the early presidents, one of the remarkable New England dynasty at Northwestern. In addition to Dr. Haven, Presidents Hinman

NATHAN SMITH DAVIS was guiding power behind medical school which became part of University in 1869.

PROMINENT FACULTY MEMBERS of early Medical School days included (left to right) Doctors Edmund Andrews, W. H. Byford, Titus DeVille, J. H. Hollister, Ralph N. Isham, Hosmer A. Johnson, F. Mahla, David Rutter, H. G. Spafford, M. R. Raylor, and Horace Wardner. They were pioneers in field of medical education.

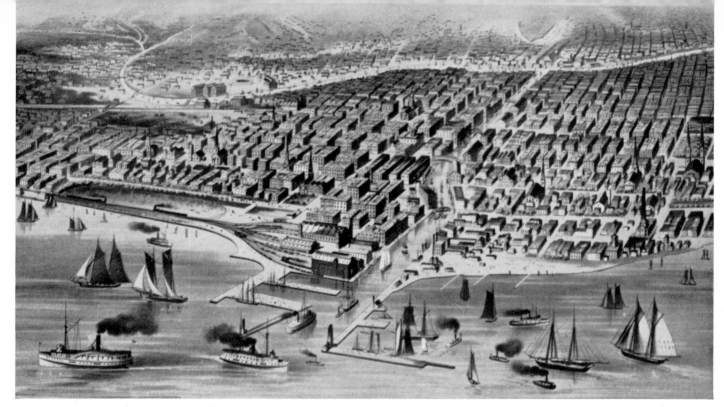

CHICAGO OF 1871 was bustling giant among midwest towns. Sketch shows Chicago shortly before great fire.

and Cummings, Acting Presidents Noyes and Marcy, and Professors Carhart, Cumnock and Bannister were all graduates of Wesleyan University at Middletown, Connecticut and several had been associated with Newbury Seminary in Newbury, Vermont.

During his years as president of the University of Michigan, Dr. Haven expressed progressive views on the subjects of women's education and the expansion of the scientific departments of the university. It was predicted that he would develop these questions at Northwestern and he did. It was under his leadership that women were admitted to the University in 1869. Dr. Haven welcomed unification with the Chicago Medical College, although the initiative for the measure was Dr. Davis' rather than his. On the other hand, the President failed to persuade the trustees to accept the one really revolutionary measure which he advocated, the establishment of a properly constituted College of Technology. Courses were begun in engineering subjects, but the project of a separate college was not adequately developed, a fact which the University was to regret during the next two decades.

Haven's administration was eventful in other respects. Luther Greenleaf presented a large and important collection of classical books and pamphlets to the library, students flocked to Professor Robert MacLean Cumnock's lectures in elocution and the Evanston College for Ladies took over the Fourth of July of 1871 to raise money for its new building. The experiment of mixed classes was begun and even the Hinman and Adelphic Societies opened their membership to the

CHICAGO WATER TOWER, finished a few years before great conflagration, survived 1871 tragedy to become a famous landmark in the Chicago of today.

CHICAGO OF 1879 SHOWS CHANGES AND GROWTH. Fire did not discourage Chicagoans, who rebuilt city.

girls. Seniors, members of the new Life-Saving Crew, practiced in their new boat under the admiring eyes of the whole University, and the ninth issue of the University student monthly, *The Tripod*, reflected the progressiveness of 1871 in its note that, "It would be a matter of general convenience and rejoicing, if the proper authorities would see to it that at least one sidewalk be constructed soon between the University building and Heck Hall. Such a convenience would be a luxury in comparison with the sand that must be waded through now by those who have occasion to ply between these points."

In the second week of October of the same year a flash of fire was seen on DeKoven Street in the teeming city of Chicago. After two days of terror the city lay in ruins and Mrs. O'Leary's cow was a part of popular legend. Evanston became a haven for refugees and *The Tripod* of November 20th noted that, "Sufferers by the fire will be provided with board, lodging, lights, fuel, washing and tuition at the Evanston College for Ladies, at very low rates. For the last half of the autumn term, and proportionally for any fraction thereof, students will be received and cared for as above for thirty-five dollars."

The finances of the University suffered con-

siderably from the fire's devastation, but frugality and initiative had built the University and they preserved it. As early as the spring of 1872, the organization of University Publishing Company with a capital of $100,000 demonstrated the strength of the University's recuperative powers. The most serious loss as a result of the fire was not, in fact, financial, but personal, since President Haven, despairing of the recovery of the University's finances,

TROLLEYS AND HORSE DRAWN carriages are seen in sketch showing busy State Street in earlier days.

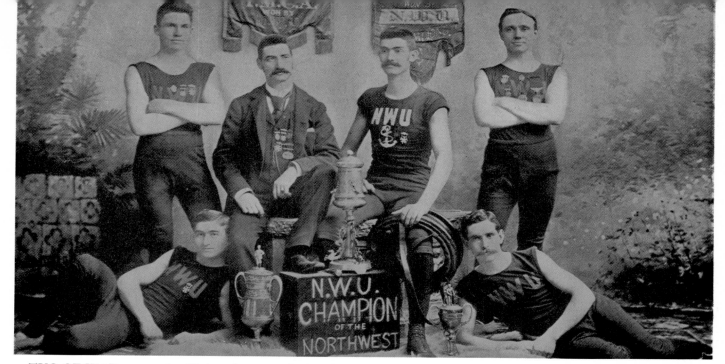

TUG OF WAR was major University sport in 1880's and 1890's.   Northwestern's championship team of 1892-93 was proud of its many trophies. Growth of football before the turn of century brought decline of rope-pulling sport.

1875—BASEBALL SQUAD won coveted championship of Northwest, obtaining first trophy for team.

resigned to become Secretary of the Methodist Board of Education. He was succeeded as president by Charles Henry Fowler, a distinguished Methodist preacher of Chicago and a graduate of Garrett Biblical Institute.

Pioneers, struggling with an unfriendly environment, are necessarily serious people. The first generation of Northwestern students was almost fully occupied with the difficult business of getting an education. In the second twenty years of Northwestern's history, however, the extracurricular activities of the students expanded rapidly.

University sports, beyond the primitive level of class riots, began to develop after the Civil War. In its third number, dated April 20, 1871, *The Tripod* noted that "the time for out-door amusements has come again, and is cordially greeted by our old baseball enthusiasts, who have lost none of their ardor in the game, but are at work energetically organizing class clubs." The 1870's were highlighted by the news of the series of baseball games for the silver ball donated by the Evanston College for Ladies, in which Northwestern was twice defeated by mighty Racine. Professor Julius Kellogg was a strong supporter of the team, both in class and out. In 1880 Northwestern was accused of employing an ineligible player. After that the league fell apart and a Western College Baseball Association

STUDENTS OF 1870's were anxious to get gym. Shares of stock were issued to those who financed construction.

TODAY'S MINERALOGICAL laboratory once served University as gymnasium. This is early photo of exterior.

continued in a desultory fashion for a decade, featured by the advent of "Billy" Sunday as Northwestern coach for a season, and by the never-to-be-forgotten championship victory over Wisconsin in 1889.

In the '90's, however, football replaced baseball as the chief college sport. Introduced at Northwestern in 1876, it did not become popular until 1887. A defeat by Notre Dame in 1889 inspired a new enthusiasm for the game, the comment being that, "what is needed is a coacher, an eminent specialist who has blocked his man in a game against Yale's or Princeton's giants." Tug-of-war was pop-

ular in the 1880's, but after achieving the Intercollegiate Championship in 1891, Northwestern gave up this strenuous sport for football. Field days were also popular, the emphasis, in these pre-conference days, being on intramural contests. Tennis was an interclass sport, and a gun club was organized in the 1870's. The ladies also developed competitions in archery and bean bag, and the gentlemen were informed that they "may look over the fence and watch the game of croquet, except on Saturday mornings when they may be permitted to tread the sacred soil and mingle in the sport." The develop-

NORTHWESTERN'S FIRST GYM was financed by students. Stocks were issued to those who financed construction.

NORTHWESTERN'S FAMOUS United States Coast Guard station was founded after Lady Elgin disaster.

ment of intercollegiate sports necessitated the adoption of school colors, and after discussion and changes, the purple and gold combination was adopted in 1879.

The Tripod commented in 1871 that "The University, with all its advantages, yet lacks one thing—a good, well-furnished permanent gymnasium." In 1876 the students took matters into their own hands, organized a joint-stock company and built a two-story frame structure on a lot north of Old College. The gymnasium, despite the attractions of a

PROUD MEN standing in front of Coast Guard station were members of early University life saving crew.

CAPTAIN LAWSON, courageous leader of life saving crew, who led them to their many heroic rescues.

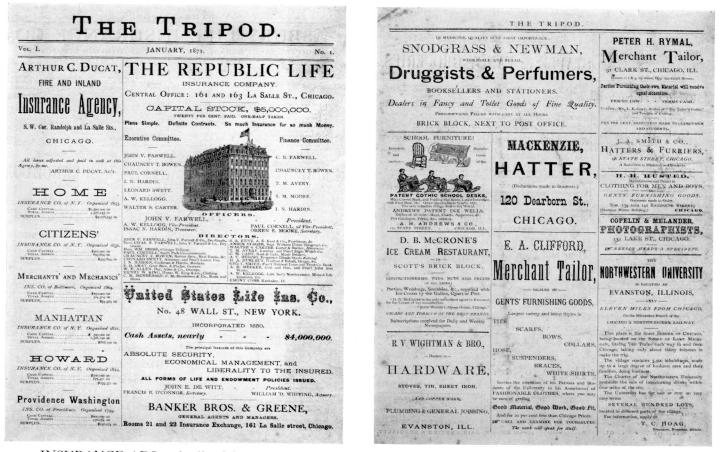

bowling alley and the latest gymnastic equipment, did not prove as popular as was expected and by 1880 could not be continued on a paying basis. In 1882 the University assumed the responsibility and a "fine-looking brick-veneered structure" was erected on the frame of the old building. New apparatus was purchased and a director put in charge. Certain hours were set aside for the use of the gymnasium by the girls, inspiring the comment that "their dejected brethren wander lugubriously around, longing for the chance to prepare themselves for the rigors of the coming baseball campaign or the arduous strifes of field-day."

Physical prowess could also be exhibited in the Life-Saving Crew. The first boat was given into the charge of the seniors (Class of '72) in October, 1871 and, despite the fact that a short-sighted government had neglected to provide either ways or a boathouse, drills were carried out with great regularity and vigor. For the first three or four years no

SELF-CONSCIOUS LADIES and gentlemen are members of *Syllabus* editorial board in early school days.

FENCE WAS ERECTED to protect lawns from carriages and cattle, major problems in the early 1880's.

CLASS OF 1873 donated this boulder, one of first class memorials. It now stands west of Harris Hall.

after it moved from the campus upon the graduation of its founders.

The second twenty years of the University's existence also saw the expansion of student societies. The student of the 1880's could debate in the Hinman or Adelphic Societies or take part in oratorical contests and inspire such comment as: "Miss Julia D. Watson, '80, in a natural and finely modulated voice, read the famous 'Henry V's Wooing' so skilfully as almost to remove the bad impression produced by white gloves and a reading stand."

WHISKERED FACULTY MEMBERS and students stand by Heck Hall, dormitory for theological students. Building was erected on present site of Deering Library in 1867 as centenary memorial of Methodist Episcopal Church.

EVANSTON WOMEN'S COLLEGE students lived and studied in this building, now home of School of Music.

The student could join the Glee Club, think deeply with the Philosophical Society or read Goethe at the German Club. The Athenaeum was open to all those "who have a taste for art or literature, or who can in any way contribute to the advancement of these ends," and the Students' Christian Association, formed in 1880, promoted the religious life of the campus. At the Friday night lectures at the Women's College, Chaplain C. C. McCabe revealed "The Dark Side of Life in Libby Prison" and Mrs. Mary Livermore set before her audience the conumdrum "What Shall We Do with Our Daughters?" Even in gradua-

REST COTTAGE, home of Miss Willard, still stands at 1730 Chicago Avenue.

FRANCES WILLARD, first dean of women at Northwestern, later national leader, W.C.T.U.

DEMPSTER HALL, men's dormitory, is shown here with two silk-hatted faculty members talking on lawn.

tion the student did not leave student societies behind, for he could then become a member of the Alumni Association and continue his relation with the University.

Parties and social evenings were increasing in number and in the 1880's the rigorous code

1882 COMMENCEMENT PROGRAM shows old oak.

YOU ARE INVITED TO ATTEND THE COMMENCEMENT EXERCISES OF THE NORTHWESTERN UNIVERSITY EVANSTON

JUNE 16TH TO JUNE 22 1882

THE OLD OAK AT UNIVERSITY GROUNDS

of propriety was so far relaxed as to permit carefully supervised dancing. The desire for organized social life was also reflected in the formation of fraternities and sororities. A chapter of Sigma Chi fraternity, founded in 1868, was the first fraternity having continuous life on the campus, although Phi Delta Theta had made an abortive appearance after 1859. Phi Kappa Sigma and Beta Theta Pi followed in 1872 and 1873. In 1880 sororities were introduced to the campus. Alpha Phi was the first, followed in 1882 by Delta Gamma and Kappa Kappa Gamma.

The new freedom of the student body gave a new meaning and strength to class rivalry. The seniors wore silk hats, the juniors white "plugs" and the freshmen demonstrated their superiority in heavy metal mortarboards. In addition to such harmless pastimes as "Burning Trig" and the cane rush, rioting, both intramural and between town and gown, was prevalent. Class elections were a favorite occasion for the exercise of militant democracy, and charges of clique voting and "fixed" elections at times led to combat. The Junior Exhibition with its learned essays and pompous poetry, until its abandonment in 1879, provided an all too favorable occasion for the destructive tendencies of sophomore

1872—COLLEGE COTTAGE, later expanded and renamed Pearsons Hall, was operated as a co-operative house for women students. Housing for women was scarce because of regulation that all must live on campus.

humor also to display themselves. Moreover, a steady stream of faculty minutes records the punishment of offenders and shows that an intermittent hostility characterized relations between the student body and the town, particularly on Halloween. Class spirit was not always expressed in assault and battery, however, as the boulder of the class of '73, the University Hall clock of the class of '79 and the University Hall bell of the class of '80 bear witness.

The new president (1872), Charles H. Fowler, despite his distinction as a theologian and public speaker, lacked experience as an educator. He also lacked the diplomatic skill of President Haven, a fact which considerably limited the success of his four years' administration. In Fowler's first six months of office, however, his plans for expansion of the institution to a real university status were carried forward with efficiency.

These plans included taking over the Evanston College for Ladies as the Women's College of the University. Fowler did not approve of his predecessor's plan of having the two institutions separate but associated, and in 1873 brought about amalgamation. Almost immediately serious friction developed between the President and Dean Willard, who, although progressive in the regulation of her students, required that they abide by strict rules concerning living quarters and conduct. The President, on the other hand, maintained that the young ladies could live where they

IN EVANSTON HOMES, such as these, all students lived before development of the quadrangle system.

HATFIELD HOUSE, dorm for 30 students, was built in 1888 with donation from Rev. R. M. Hatfield.

pleased and abide by only those rules which applied to all students. The controversy took on a new interest for the onlookers when it was remembered that Miss Willard had once been engaged to marry The Reverend Mr. Fowler. The struggle of wills was soon over, however, and Dean Willard resigned in 1874. She was succeeded by Ellen M. Soule, and shortly thereafter by Jane Bancroft.

The rules of the Women's College required that all women students should live in residence. It resulted that accommodation for women students was scarce, despite the recent completion of the new Women's College building which was later named Willard Hall. One attempt to meet this shortage was the purchase in 1872 of College Cottage, at the corner of Clark Street and Orrington Avenue. Here a successful experiment in cooperative living was established, but even this proved inadequate, and the pressure for accommodation was not really relieved until the expansion of College Cottage into Pearsons Hall, named in honor of Mrs. John A. Pearsons, in 1890, and the addition of Chapin Hall in 1902.

Men's living quarters were also much in demand. The Club House, built in 1865, had space for only twenty and Heck Hall housed only theological students. The acquisi-

tion of Dempster Hall in 1874 was of some assistance, until the building was destroyed by fire in 1879, but the overwhelming majority of the men students boarded in private homes or student clubs until the development of the North Campus houses in the twentieth century.

In other respects President Fowler's administration was a time of progress. In 1859 the tentative beginnings of a law school had been made with the appointment of Judge Henry Booth as dean and the beginning of classwork in rented rooms at the corner of Clark and Washington Streets in Chicago. In 1873 President Fowler and the trustees entered into a contract to cooperate with the old University of Chicago in maintaining the school under the title of Union College of Law. Two years was to constitute the regular course and it was recommended that law be undertaken only as a graduate study. In the late 1880's the first University of Chicago collapsed because of lack of funds, and in 1891 Northwestern assumed the full cost of the Union College which became Northwestern University Law School.

Plans for the establishment of a College of Technology were outlined in Dr. Fowler's report to the trustees for 1873. Because of

BID TO THETA NU EPSILON, sophomore men's honorary, was considered great distinction for men of 1890's.

1877—CLASS OF UNION COLLEGE OF LAW.   In 1890's college became Northwestern Law School.

the nature of the studies, an organization for faculty and students separate from the main University was recommended, and a small grant of *$2,500* a year was proposed, to be raised from outside sources. Four-year courses in engineering, chemistry, and natural history were planned and a faculty of eleven was appointed. Professor Marcy was to serve as dean, and Professor Henry Carhart, who had already demonstrated his genius by the installation of a system of electric bells in University Hall, became professor of physics. The College was begun on a wave of optimism but the great depression of the 1870's destroyed any hope of solid financial backing, and the experiment was discontinued in 1877.

Meanwhile the curriculum of Liberal Arts had been improved. Modern language studies were regularized and the degree of Bachelor of Letters was instituted. In 1874 requirements for the degree of Master of Arts were increased to include graduate study in residence, rather than the mere possession of a bachelor's degree and a good character. In the same year the granting of the degree of Doctor of Philosophy was tentatively offered and then withdrawn, to be instituted eighteen years later. A Conservatory of Music was organized in the Women's College in 1872 and in 1877 it was placed on a permanent basis with Oren E. Locke as director. The Preparatory Department, on which the University relied for

the training of most of its local students, was also expanded under the leadership of Herbert Franklin Fisk, the new principal, appointed in 1875.

On the evidence of Dr. Marcy, the University during these four years "had risen from a very small college to one of the largest universities in the country." In May, 1876, the architect of this progress, Dr. Fowler, resigned, to become editor of the *New York Christian Advocate*. It was the third occasion on which a University president had been appointed to a high Methodist post, and Dr. Marcy, Fowler's acting successor, voiced the resentment of the University when he declared: "The public sentiment in our Church is wrong in this matter. It places any General Conference appointment superior to the presidency of our colleges. The college cannot rise higher than the man who is kept at its head." The practice was not repeated after 1876.

Dr. Marcy's administration began in an atmosphere of debts and deficits, for the full effects of the great depression were just making themselves felt. The necessary expansion undertaken during President Fowler's regime had been carried out partially on credit which was later withdrawn. Faculty salaries were again in arrears, unproductive land was sold and lessees of University property were forced to cancel. Even building repairs had to be neglected and the Lunt Library Fund was

41

diverted to general purposes, despite the protests of the faculty. When a number of the faculty resigned the University lacked the means to replace them and, as Dr. Marcy pointed out, "To place Logic in the hands of the Professor of Natural History and Rhetoric in charge of the Professor of Civil Engineering, and have the work well done could not reasonably be expected."

Such reductions in facilities, and particularly the abolition of the College of Technology, handicapped the University in the very sharp competition of colleges for students and further reduced its revenue. A more serious threat to the University's existence came with the famous tax case of 1874-79.

Marcy. The attorneys for the City charged that the trustees used the tax exemption for private gain. The trustees themselves expressed their profound relief at the preservation of the University.

This was not the only cause for satisfaction during these troubled years. The library, numbering more than 30,000 books and pamphlets, including the Greenleaf collection of classical and modern literature and a government documents section, was the most complete in the Middle West. The new College of Medicine, unlike the University, was in an extremely prosperous condition. A new emphasis was being laid upon graduate work throughout the University, inspired in part by

Oliver Marcy
Acting President
1876-1881

Joseph Cummings
President
1881-1890

The controversial amendment of 1855 to the University's charter, which had exempted University property from taxation, had already been unsuccessfully challenged in 1867. This second attempt on the part of the City of Evanston to obtain revenue from the University was far more serous, since the Illinois Supreme Court decided against the University, leaving the trustees to reflect that "If the suit is lost it will be equal to a mortgage of $150,000 at six per cent on our property." The Supreme Court of the United States, to which the case was appealed, held, however, that the charter amendment was valid. When the good news was received student bonfires blazed with the special permission of President

the opening of the Johns Hopkins University in 1876. In 1878 the Cumnock School of Oratory was established. Under Professor Robert MacLean Cumnock, this distinguished and unique institution continued for sixteen years to provide several generations of students with a useful and inspiring education in public speaking and literary interpretation. Until it was transferred from its quarters in University Hall in 1895 to the present School of Speech, the School remained autonomous, but affiliated with the University.

There were signs, by 1879, that the University was slowly drawing clear of the financial difficulties which had beset it during Dr. Marcy's regime. In 1881 a drive was begun for $200,000 to free the University from debt. The drive was a complete success, due in large part to the $100,000 donation of Dr. Evans, and donations from others, including a gift of $25,000 from William A. Deering.

Building and Consolidation, 1881–1890

The new prosperity was especially welcome to Dr. Marcy, since it enabled him in 1881 to retire from the acting presidency and to return to scientific pursuits. The *Northwestern* had already demanded that a successor to Dr. Marcy be appointed, "a man to whom the

University's deficit was almost wiped out and the rent roll had increased through the expansion of Evanston onto hitherto unproductive University property. In addition, the freshman class of 1881 was the largest in the history of the University and revenue was more than adequate to meet expenditure. Once again the faculty enjoyed full salaries and these were now paid on a monthly basis. There were also additions to the faculty, including a number of former graduates. Charles W. Pearson, Arts '71, became professor of English literature and history, and Robert Baird, Arts '70, was professor of Greek. Professor Robert D. Sheppard, a graduate of Garrett Biblical Institute, became the first

Early diploma.

University seal.

students will look with confidence, a man who will be able to command respect, to compel obedience, to so marshal our hosts as to insure a grand and glorious victory. We need a man whose breadth of thought, exactness of scholarship, soundness of judgment, determination and zeal will gain for him recognition abroad as well as at home." Since Dr. Marcy's successor, Dr. Joseph Cummings, was extremely popular with the students, it is to be presumed that he met at least some of these exacting requirements.

Cummings, a distinguished former president of Wesleyan University, had a generally successful administration. He was fortunate in the times. Prosperity had returned, the

professor of history and political economy, and Dean Bancroft was succeeded as dean of the Women's College by Miss Rena A. Michaels.

Many of the refinements of a mature university were instituted during this period. The faculty puzzled for many years over the problems presented by the Latin inscriptions on diplomas, describing Northwestern as "Universitatis Caurinae" or "Universitatis Evanstoniensis," finally deciding in favor of the present English inscription of "Northwestern University" and a committee under Dr. Bonbright designed a University seal with the inscription *Quaecumque sunt vera*. The Liberal Arts course was divided into general and

1888—FAYERWEATHER HALL was completed. Daniel B. Fayerweather was donor of building which an enthusiastic admirer called "one of the finest and most perfectly adapted buildings of its kind." It was pride of campus.

honors categories. Such student comment as "we don't want drivers for teachers, we want guides. But the recitations we can best do without are those in which the time is spent in quizzing," indicated that the honors course was at first unpopular. The prominence which the honors students acquired in the University soon changed this attitude, however. The spirit of mature student criticism was also reflected in the condemnation of an exasperating faculty practice in regard to required reading. "One of the professors advises us to read certain books which may be found in the library. Then said professor goes straightway and procures the books, takes them to his room and keeps them during the term we are pursuing said study."

The founding of the Illinois Alpha Chapter of Phi Beta Kappa on the campus in 1889 was a reflection of the desire to improve

1884, MEMORIAL HALL originally served Garrett Biblical Institute. Now School of Commerce.

1881—CLASS OF MEDI-
CAL SCHOOL grouped at
entrance to Mercy Hospital
on Calumet Avenue. Dr.
Nathan Davis (with high
silk hat) stands in center.

scholastic standards, as well as evidence that Northwestern, first of the midwestern universities to be honored by membership, was coming of age. The numbers to be selected from each graduating class were not to exceed one-fourth of the membership of the class and women were not admitted until 1892. The weekly *Northwestern*, in condemning this early exclusion of women, pointed to the University's progressive coeducational tradition and stated, "if a woman enters the same course, pursues it with the same credit and attains the same standards with a man, we can find no argument neither in reason nor

SHEPPARD FIELD, first Northwestern stadium, was scene of many football struggles before turn of century.

EVANSTON CITIZENS WHO TRAVELED to Niagara Falls in 1890 included Dr. Oliver Marcy (at right).

OLD OAK, WOOD FENCE, horse drawn carts gave flavor of 1880's to southwest corner of campus.

in justice which should prevent her from sharing equally with a man in the crowning honor."

The chief need of the University during the 1880's was unification. Despite the small-scale improvements undertaken, there was a serious falling off in registration, particularly in the College of Liberal Arts. If Northwestern was to compete successfully with the state universities and the heavily-endowed private institutions of the East, less expensive

VIEW OF SHADED SOUTH CAMPUS, Fayerweather Hall, Preparatory School, and Life Saving Station.

education and more facilities, particularly in the newly-popular scientific fields, must be offered. It was a time of great developments in the physical equipment of universities.

In 1886 Daniel B. Fayerweather made a donation for the erection of a hall of science, "not only the most perfect and most handsome of the University buildings, but one of the finest and most perfectly adapted buildings of its kind in the United States," according to enthusiastic student comment. The new addition, Fayerweather Hall, quite outshone the previous pride of the campus, the Memorial Hall of Garrett Biblical Institute, completed in 1884. University facilities were being expanded in other directions also.

In 1886 the Illinois College of Pharmacy became affiliated with the University under Dean Oscar Oldberg and Dr. John H. Long. Its quarters at 40 Dearborn Street in Chicago were reported by the *Chicago Daily News* to be the best equipped in the country and its requirements for graduation compared very favorably with the standards of the best pharmacy schools then existing.

The University catalogue for 1887-88 noted

THREE 1882 GRADUATES: James Conwell, member of Life Saving Crew; Evan Evans, son of founder, and William Dyche, future "N.U." Business Manager.

another addition, with the announcement that a College of Dental and Oral Surgery (University Dental College) had been established. Students were required to take a three year's course of twenty-one months before graduation, the College being the first dental school in the country to set such a high standard. Its affiliation with the University was nominal, on much the same basis as that

Above—GEORGE WASHINGTON HOUGH became director of Dearborn Observatory at opening in 1889.

Center—CONSTRUCTION OF OBSERVATORY was made possible by J. B. Hobbs' large donation.

Below—WELL-KNOWN ASTRONOMERS of 1880's visiting Evanston in honor of Dearborn opening.

STUDENTS OF 1880's took time from studies to have fun. This is typical costume party of period.

of Chicago Medical College. The Dental College was not a financial success, however, and in 1891 the University assumed direct control.

In 1887, students could be heard shouting the remarkable question "Who was the first man?" to which the answer was "J. B. Hobbs," who had recently donated $25,000 for the erection of an observatory to house what was described as "the ninth largest telescope in the whole world." The idea of the observatory was not new but had grown out of the organization of the Chicago Astronomical Society in 1862. In 1873 this Society went bankrupt as a result of the Chicago Fire and a contract was made with Northwestern University for the transfer of the eighteen and one-half inch telescope to Northwestern's campus as soon as a suitable building was erected. The contribution of Mr. Hobbs in 1887 made possible the fulfillment of the contract. The Dearborn Observatory, under the direction of Professor George Washington ("Jupiter") Hough, was opened in 1889, replacing the "neat little shanty without varnish or gilt . . . made of the plaster-boards left over when the Women's College was built," which had served hitherto as the headquarters of the Astronomical Department.

The last year of President Cummings' administration was one of marked prosperity. A large increase in the University's revenue was in prospect through the revaluation of its Chicago property, and the student registration of nearly 2,500 was the largest in the University's history. The problem for the immediate future appeared to be the closer union of the various elements of the University. This was not to be the work of President Cummings. He had been in poor health for three years. The burden of supervising the many details, both administrative and academic, of his office was too arduous for him and on May 7, 1890, he died. The administration of Dr. Cummings marks the end of the first period of the University's growth.

Forty years had seen the foundations laid. A university, neither narrowly sectarian nor irreligious, but broadly liberal with a definite religious emphasis, had been founded. It was an institution designed to serve not merely Chicago or the state of Illinois or the Methodist community, but all the people of the vast Northwest Territory. It set high standards of scholarship in keeping with the ideals envisaged by such men as Dr. Evans, President Hinman and Professor Bonbright. These ideals were a heritage which was to prove more valuable than the material assets of the University.

A high standard had been set in the business affairs of Northwestern. In an era when many colleges were failing after only a few years of existence, Northwestern had had a history of difficult but steady expansion which wars and depressions had barely interrupted. From the beginnings in 1855 of one frame building the physical equipment had grown to include five major buildings on the Evanston campus and a number of buildings in Chicago. Four professional schools, which were to develop in succeeding decades into some of the finest in the country, had become affiliated with Northwestern. In 1890 the University was still a congeries of autonomous schools but the groundwork had been laid on which a consolidated structure could be built. A new era was about to begin.

GROWTH AND CONSOLIDATION
1890-1920

GROWTH AND CONSOLIDATION
1890-1920

Henry Wade Rogers, President, 1890-1900

A decade was left in the nineteenth century, but for Northwestern University, as for much of the rest of the world, a new era was already beginning. The uncertain light of electricity illuminated many homes and the new experiment of the electric train was the subject of grave misgivings on the part of officials in eastern cities. Skyscrapers and typewriters were rapidly becoming familiar in the business life of Chicago. The Gibson Girl appeared and gentlemen exchanged the whiskers of the middle of the century for the more modest mustache. It was an age of progress.

In his speech at the installation of the new president in 1890, Dean Nathan Smith Davis predicted the influence which the new era was to have on higher education. "The . . . application of scientific knowledge to such inventions and devices as foster every art and every branch of human industry, have so quickened human thought that it can no longer move in the educational grooves and ruts of the past without constant friction."

Daniel Bonbright, President, 1900-1902

The Rogers Administration, 1890-1900

It is not surprising, therefore, that in terms of change and development in the University, the administration of Dr. Henry Wade Rogers was one of the most important in Northwestern's history. The reorientation of the University was unobtrusive but profound. In 1890 the intellectual emphasis at Northwestern was distinctly religious, with the administration predomi-

CAMPUS BUILDINGS included first north quad, Medical School, Prep School, Patten Gym, Dental School and business office.

Edmund Janes James, President, 1902-1904

51

1893-94—UNIVERSITY'S FACULTY in Evanston included: (first row) Emily Wheeler, James Hatfield, George Hough, A. V. E. Young, Henry Rogers (president), Herbert Fisk, John Gray, H. B. Loomis; (second row) Henry Stanclift, Henry Cohn, Thomas Holgate, John Clark, Charles Atwell, Daniel Bonbright, Oliver Marcy; (third row) B. S. Annis, Henry White, Henry Crew, George Coe, Alja Crook, Robert Baird, and Charles Labeaud.

nantly in the hands of Methodist laymen. By 1900 the emphasis was more academic and the influence of the nation's new industrial and mercantile leadership more pronounced. The personnel recruited for the faculty was also different. Until 1890 Wesleyan University had supplied a large proportion of the faculty.

LAKE ATWELL, south of "U.H.," more campus beauty.

In the new regime Ph.D.'s of Johns Hopkins University were prominent and the change brought with it a new emphasis on the purposes and requirements of higher education, particularly in regard to graduate studies.

Almost immediately after his inauguration the new president turned his attention to the problem of strengthening the faculty. The professors appointed during Dr. Rogers' administration were among the finest to be found. The noteworthy group from the Johns Hopkins included Henry Crew, in physics; James Taft Hatfield, in German literature; Grant Conklin, in zoology; John A. Scott, in Greek; Omera Floyd Long in Latin and James A. James in history.

No opportunity was lost, moreover, to supplement their services with those of the best products of both American and European universities. John H. Gray, in economics and political science, from Halle; Henry White and Thomas Franklin Holgate, in mathematics, from Clark University; William A. Locy, in zoology, from the University of Chicago, and George A. Coe, in philosophy, from the University of Berlin. These men built their lives into the University, becoming nationally prominent scholars in their fields and leaders in the development of the University.

Other changes came rapidly. The courses of the junior and senior years in the College of Liberal Arts became almost entirely elective. Separate departments were established for history, political science and economics, and an old dream came closer to realization with the acquisition of funds for a College of Engineering, largely through the Fayerweather bequest and a donation by William Deering.

As a trained lawyer, President Rogers placed a new and greater stress on the business and organizational aspects of the University, an emphasis foreshadowed in his inaugural statement: "It is my belief that when the spirit of progress demands it, conservatism ought not to stand in the way of such changes as tend to be in the best interests of the University." Almost immediately the president established an office in Chicago. It was a portent of other progressive measures. Despite the fact that Northwestern was now the third largest university in the nation in terms of student enrollment, the idea of the University still centered on the College of Liberal Arts, with the professional schools only loosely affiliated.

In 1891 the consolidation of the governing boards of the various colleges into a central board of trustees for the whole University

1895—UNIVERSITY DENTAL SCHOOL and American College of Dental Surgery were consolidated.

and the creation of a University Council for interfaculty affairs helped to centralize the institution. Some of the hitherto autonomous colleges assumed the name of Northwestern and the University became much more closely identified with the city of Chicago. Distinguished members of the faculty also did their

1890—SHERIDAN ROAD had no pavement but more trees than it has today. Some homes at left still stand.

1891—DR. PETER LUTKIN, named Director of Conservatory of Music when it became part of University.

monies themselves, for they now featured the wearing of academic cap and gown by the graduating class and faculty and the delivery of a baccalaureate address by the president, in place of the customary sermon.

The chief problem in the reorganization of the University was, as usual, money. It was a time of great developments in the physical equipment of universities. The new industrial giants were investing in education, particularly technological education, and the chief topic of academic conversation in the early 1890's was John D. Rockefeller's two-million dollar endowment of the new Baptist University of Chicago.

President Rogers, in his inaugural address, stated Northwestern's needs for the future: "The duty, therefore, is to increase our endowment more rapidly than the educational institutions of the East are increasing theirs, if we hope ever to equal them in the educational advantages we can offer." Fortunately the first years of Dr. Rogers' administration were prosperous, and the facilities of the University were expanded.

Through the energetic support of Miss Cornelia Lunt, the daughter of Orrington Lunt, the Conservatory of Music, which had not been an organic part of the University, was affiliated in 1891. Dr. Peter Christian Lutkin, organist and composer, was appointed

duty as citizens by devoting their talents to the solution of problems of administration, public health and building in Chicago, and the city took pride in the achievements of its oldest university. This bond was dramatized by the removal of commencement exercises in 1892 from the First Methodist Church in Evanston to the Chicago Auditorium Theater. Changes were also made in the cere-

1897—MUSIC SCHOOL got new building on University Place; now used as practice hall for music students.

1894—LUNT LIBRARY was constructed to house 100,000 books. Orrington Lunt gave $50,000 toward building.

its director and under his inspired leadership the Conservatory rapidly became one of the foremost schools in the country. However, it was not raised to the status of a permanent school until 1895. The trustees regarded the study of music as something of a luxury, and proper building accommodation was lacking. It was largely due to the leadership and force of character of Peter Lutkin that this problem was overcome with the completion of the Hall of Music on University Place in 1897. Dr. Lutkin became dean of the new school, an office to which he lent distinction for more than a quarter of a century.

The financial panic of 1893-94 affected progress only slightly. Even the lapse of the Grand Pacific Hotel's lease of the University's LaSalle Street property in Chicago was compensated by a new long-term lease of the property by the Illinois Trust Company. Despite small deficits in some of the schools and a falling-off in the registration of students, plans for expansion were still pursued.

In his first report to the trustees President Rogers had stated: "A library building which will hold 100,000 volumes should be provided as soon as possible and liberal provision should be made from year to year for the purchase of books." Fortunately the recommendation could be carried out. The twenty-five year old Orrington Lunt Library Fund was augmented by a further gift of $50,000 by Mr. Lunt in 1891 and an additional $50,000 from various sources, raised through the efforts of the Rev. Robert Hatfield. In September, 1894, the new Orrington Lunt Library was dedicated

MISS CORNELIA LUNT, daughter of Orrington Lunt, gave strong support to Conservatory of Music.

55

1895—ANNIE MAY SWIFT HALL, gift of Gustavus F. Swift, was constructed to house School of Oratory.

with a "notable address" on "The Development of the Library" by Justin Winsor, eminent librarian of Harvard University.

In May, 1895, the Annie May Swift Hall of Oratory was opened. This Venetian structure of buff Roman brick and terra cotta, a "poem in stone" in the words of Frances Willard, was the gift of Gustavus F. Swift and named in memory of his deceased daughter, a former student at Northwestern. Its construction marked the fulfillment of the life-long dream of Director Robert MacLean Cumnock, of creating a properly constituted school "to prepare men for oratory in the senate, at the bar, on the platform and in the pulpit; for interpretation of literature in public and in private; for professional teaching in the school; for reading in the home."

One year earlier the Cumnock School of Oratory had become affiliated with the University as Northwestern School of Oratory. Director Cumnock was to have exclusive right to nominate all instructors and to determine the general policy of the School, subject to final confirmation by the University trustees. In 1895 the School's course of study was expanded by offering one year of graduate study.

Forensic activities had flourished on the campus for many years, under the aegis of the School of Oratory. As early as 1873 Northwestern was participating in debates with the University of Chicago and in 1899 began to take part in intercollegiate debates sponsored by the Central Debating League (later the Western Conference Debating League). The annual Kirk Oratorical Contest was endowed by John B. Kirk in 1877. In addition, in 1890 the University began its participation in the contests of the Northern Oratorical League. Other activities of the School at this time included sponsoring dramatics organizations such as the Prentice Players, the Campus Players and the Thalian Dramatic Club. The success of the School, which remained one of the most respected institutions of this type, was due primarily to the energy and teaching skill of Cumnock, who was one of the great teachers of speech in America.

There were also other improvements on the Evanston campus. Steam heating was installed in University Hall and the campus was enclosed by an iron fence, the gift of William Deering. The fence had become necessary because, in the words of the trustees, "the

LOUNGE in Annie May Swift Hall provided place for relaxation and conversation for School of Oratory.

AUDITORIUM SERVED as laboratory and show place for students in University's School of Oratory.

conduct of certain persons from the town has become a nuisance." During the decade another building was added. The preparatory school, or Academy as it was now called, acquired the new Fisk Hall, again through the generosity of William Deering. This was a welcome addition to the campus, for not only had the Academy outgrown its quarters in the Old College, but the chapel of the new building, with a seating capacity of eight hundred, could be used as an assembly hall.

In these years profound changes were being made in the curricula of the various schools, in line with President Rogers' plan for a well-integrated University. Northwestern established a Summer School on a permanent basis in 1892 and adopted the semester plan for the academic year in 1897. In the following year the reorganization of the Women's College of the University brought with it the creation

1898—FISK Hall was built to serve as headquarters for Northwestern preparatory school, now Academy.

1903—STUDENTS experimented in medical and physiological chemistry laboratory of University Medical School.

of the office of the dean of women.

In this second period of the University's development the professional schools, which have contributed so greatly to the University's distinction in the field of higher education, really developed. The Medical School had gained repute before 1890. Dr. Nathan Smith Davis, founder and first dean, had also been one of the founders of the American Medical Association and served as chairman of the International Medical Congress at London in 1889. In addition to the brilliant work of other faculty members such as Dr. Christian Fenger, authority on surgery, the Medical School became famous through the work of such alumni as Drs. Isaac Abt, Frank Billings and Charles H. Mayo. Northwestern Medical School was the first institution in the United States to establish a graded course of medical instruction, to insist upon preliminary university education for the students of medicine and to require a three years' course

STUDENTS AND PATIENTS used facilities of Davis Hall, Wesley Hospital, and Medical School Building.

"THIS IS LAW" WAS SLOGAN of celebrating law students on bunting-covered wagon in parade.

of study as a condition of graduation. In 1892 it became possible to increase the number of courses offered to students when the school extended the period of instruction to four years, being one of the first in the country to do so. In 1894 a laboratory building was added to the facilities and in 1895 the Nathan Smith Davis professorship of physiology was endowed.

The Law School was equally successful. Professor John H. Wigmore, who came to the Law School in 1893 and became its dean in 1901, was the leading authority on evidence in the country. Also of national distinction were Frederic C. Woodward, founder of the Order of the Coif, and Charles Cheney Hyde, authority on international law. In 1896 the Law School became one of the first in the United States requiring a course of three years for graduation, despite the fact that the Illinois Supreme Court had ignored the recommendations of the American Bar As-

STUDENTS STUDIED in old Law School library.

CLASSROOM for law students was in Tremont House.

FIRST NORTHWESTERN
Dental School faculty discussed
problems with Dean G. V. Black.

sociation that this requirement should be made mandatory. In 1897, however, the recommendation was accepted, largely through the influence of the Northwestern Law School.

After a protracted series of negotiations the Northwestern University Dental School and the American College of Dental Surgery were consolidated in 1895. Dr. Theodore Menges, former head of the American College of Dental Surgery, became secretary and business man-

DENTAL CLINIC in Medical School Building offered free treatment to patients for practice of dental students.

LARGE BRICK BUILDING located at corner of Madison and Franklin streets housed University Dental School.

ager of the reorganized Dental School. Among the new faculty, the most distinguished member was Dr. Greene Vardiman Black. Dr. Black had already lectured at Northwestern. He had become a world authority on dentistry and at least two of his publications, *The Formation of Poison by Micro-Organisms* (1844) and *Dental Anatomy* (1891) were standard reference works. He had also devised the first cord-driven, foot-power dental machine

LATER DENTAL CLINIC was situated in Tremont House at Lake and Dearborn.

1897—DOCTOR Greene V. Black became dean of Dental School.

GEORGE OLIVER CURME was distinguished professor of German.

PHYSICS PROFESSOR Henry Crew did research on electric arc.

and had conducted many scientific studies. On becoming dean of the Dental School in 1897, Dr. Black was faced with the task of systematizing its work. Courses of study were graded, closer personal contact between teachers and students was insured through the separation of classes into sections, and each department was brought under the control of a responsible professor. What had been a small dental school with meager facilities had become by 1900, under the leadership of the "father of modern dentistry," one of the largest and most widely known institutions of its kind.

No subject received more careful consideration by President Rogers than the need to organize graduate studies on a plane in keeping with Northwestern's high standards in

BANJOS AND MANDOLINS were popular with Northwestern men of 1890's. Club was formed for players.

1890's—GENERAL CAMPUS VIEW, looking south, showed Orrington Lunt Library, Heck Hall, and meadow.

other fields. Graduate work at the University was a matter of evolution from the early use of seminar methods in the departments of mathematics and chemistry to the organization of research plans in most other departments by 1895. The history of graduate work at Northwestern really began in 1892, however, with the registration of six graduates in residence. In 1896 the first degrees of Doctor of Philosophy were awarded at Northwestern to Vernon J. Hall and Francis C. Lockwood in chemistry and philosophy, respectively. A year later a Committee on Graduate Studies, composed of three faculty members, was established under the chairmanship of Professor Daniel Bonbright.

Northwestern's first generation of leaders had almost disappeared. Dr. Evans and Orrington Lunt, two of the most honored founders, died in 1897, and Dr. Marcy two years after. Another distinguished career ended with the retirement of Dean Nathan S. Davis in 1898. But a new generation was rising to take the place of the old. Professor George Oliver Curme joined the department of German in

1896-97 as a temporary replacement for Professor James T. Hatfield on leave of absence. In subsequent years, as professor of German philology, no less than as the author of a great German historical grammar, Dr. Curme helped to make Northwestern's German department one of the most distinguished university language departments in North America. Other faculty members were equally noteworthy in their fields and memorable as teachers, like the philosophy professor who regularly commanded his students in recitation to "Stand upon your legs and tell us a bit."

A special feature of the president's reports during the 1890's was the presentation of the intellectual activity of the University. Dr. Rogers himself was chairman of the Saratoga Conference on the Foreign Policy of the United States in 1898, author of *The Law of Expert Testimony* (1891) and associate editor of *Johnson's Universal Cyclopedia*. The University itself received recognition in 1893 with the meeting in University Hall of mathematicians from leading American and Euro-

MRS. ROGERS, active wife of president, was closely connected with University Settlement and Guild.

pean universities. This meeting, the outgrowth of the International Congress on Mathematics and Astronomy at the World's Columbian Exposition, developed into what was known as the Evanston Colloquium, to study the most important recent developments in mathematical sciences under the leadership of Professor Felix Klein of Göttingen University. So important was the work of this colloquium and that of a second, held in 1896, that the national mathematical organization, the New York Mathematical Society, changed its name to the American Mathematical Society in recognition of the work done by the western universities, particularly Northwestern. Professors Henry Seeley White and Thomas Franklin Holgate were influential in founding the Chicago section of the American Mathematical Society and in publishing the first *Transactions of the American Mathematical Society*.

Mathematics was not the only field of distinction. The American Academy of Arts and Sciences made grants to aid Professor Henry Crew in his research on the nature of the electric arc and a great Northwestern scientist was remembered in the dedication of the

Marcy Room of the marine biological laboratory at Wood's Hole, Massachusetts. In 1895 there was held in President Rogers' office an educational conference of importance to the entire Middle West. The "Presidents' Conference," which was attended by the presidents of the Universities of Michigan, Chicago, Wisconsin, Illinois, Missouri, Indiana and Ohio, had as its purpose the standardizing of the requirements for entrance to the colleges of the Middle West and the establishment of courses of instruction in accredited secondary schools which would satisfy those requirements. An Association of Colleges and Secondary Schools of the North Central States was formed, of which President Rogers was vice-president for Illinois.

Two important extracurricular organizations were founded in 1892, both on the initiative of the talented and charming Mrs. Rogers. The purpose of the University Guild was to promote interest in the University and if possible secure a fund for the erection of an art gallery and museum building. It also sponsored lectures on cultural subjects by eminent men and women from both the United States and Europe. Miss Nina Gray

1900—UNIVERSITY QUARTETTE members rested vocal chords to pose before scholarly looking volumes.

1893—WORLD COLUMBIAN EXPOSITION. View of fairgrounds showed Agricultural building across lagoon.

Lunt was the first president of the Guild, being succeeded by Mrs. Rogers in 1895.

The second of these organizations was the Northwestern University Settlement. In the 1890's American universities began to turn their attention to the appalling social conditions in the major industrial cities. The first "settlement" in Chicago under the distinct patronage of a university was Northwestern's Evanston Hall, begun in the seventeenth ward by the Northwestern University Settlement Association in 1892. Charles N. Zeublin, '87, was the chief organizer of the association, and through the efforts of Mrs. Rogers a gift was secured for the erection of an adequate building for the Settlement, Milton H. Wilson being the largest donor. Gradually the activities of the Settlement were expanded to include physical training, social clubs, music and entertainment as well as the basic relief undertakings.

Extracurricular clubs and societies of an academic nature developed extensively during the 1890's. Student organizations to promote the study of astronomy, mathematics, geology, botany, chemistry, mineralogy and physics were founded and student lecture courses sponsored eminent public figures as speakers from outside the University. William McKinley addressed the alumni on "The Value of a University Education," and William Jennings Bryan spoke to the select audience of the History Club on "The Value of an Ideal." Frances Willard made her last public address in Evanston in 1897 with her "Reminiscences of My Life at Northwestern."

The 1890's were full of stirring events in which Northwestern shared, of which the World's Columbian Exposition, held at Chicago in 1893, was one. Extensive preparations were made by the Alumni Association for the greatest reunion of graduates in the history of the University, and a holiday was granted the students so that they could attend the Exposition. Northwestern contributed in many ways to the success of the exhibitions, particularly through the services of Lyman J. Gage, trustee of the University, as president of the Exposition. President Rogers acted as chairman of the committees on law reform and higher education. In addition, Dr. Nathan Smith Davis was chairman of the committee on general medicine and surgery and Dr. John H. Long was chairman of the com-

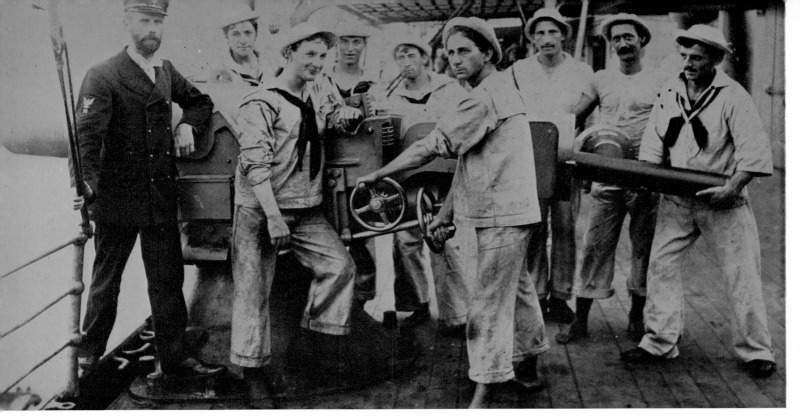

1898—PROFESSOR JAMES HATFIELD enlisted to lead gun crew on U.S.S. *Yale* during Spanish American War.

mittee on chemistry. After the great show was over valuable contributions came from it by gift and purchase to the University Museum and the University Guild's art collection. The Exposition also brought distinguished visitors from all parts of the country, among them United States Civil Service Commissioner Theodore Roosevelt, who was Northwestern's commencement speaker and who then received his first honorary LL.D.

The following year brought visitors of another kind when Coxey's Army mobilized for its protest march on Washington and a cavalry troop camped on the Evanston campus, prepared to enforce a court injunction against the Pullman strikers. Four years later world events crowded in on the University again, as patriotic young men shouted "Remember the Maine," bands informed enthusiastic crowds that "There'll Be a Hot Time in the Old Town Tonight," and Professor James Taft Hatfield of the German department left to become seaman, translator and captain of a gun's crew on the U.S.S. *Yale* during the Spanish-American War. Despite such demonstrations as a university resolution in support of the government's intervention in Cuba, the organization of a University drill squad and the rush to the colors of thirty students, the war did not greatly influence the life of the University. With the beginning of the academic year in September, 1898, life was back to normal.

Student social life was coming into its own in the 1890's. Religious interests among the

THEODORE ROOSEVELT, then United States Civil Service Commissioner, commencement speaker in 1893.

students were cultivated by two Christian Associations, and a new form of chapel service was introduced in 1896 including monthly Sunday afternoon addresses by outstanding ministers of different denominations. A University band, numbering seventeen members, was organized in 1898. As a member of the "most select and compact oratorical association ever organized in this country," the Northwestern Oratorical League, Northwestern University gained a notable place in intercollegiate forensics.

Deru, the honorary society which still performs an important function in campus life, was organized in 1898. Meanwhile fraternities and sororities gained a predominance in campus life which inspired the organization of the anti-fraternity society, Massassoits, and its publication of the *Northwestern World* in competition with the weekly *Northwestern*. The growing social sophistication of the students was also reflected in the increased number of elaborate student entertainments and in the restrictions placed on them by the administration, particularly following the introduction of the Inter-Fraternity Ball in 1895.

Relations between the students and the faculty were, on the whole, harmonious. Problems were created by the abolition of the brutal cane rush and by such exhibitions of individual enterprise as the decoration of the campus sidewalks with large vermilion '98's, in an excess of class enthusiasm. Relations with the town were also sometimes strained, as on the occasion of the disruption of a dog and pony show by gentlemen of the University in the spring of 1897. On the other hand, a happier spirit was reflected in the precedent-breaking student reception for Dr. and Mrs. Rogers in 1891 and in the formation of a Joint Committee on College Ethics, composed of five faculty and ten student members, to deal with problems which "relate to the maintenance of order and the promotion of the physical and moral health of the student community." It was hoped for a time that a student court to try cases of cribbing might serve a useful function, but the plan collapsed after two years, since the court had been unable to discover any cases to judge.

The most spectacular feature of student life in the nineties was undoubtedly the football team. Interest in the sport was greatly

UNIVERSITY BAND of 1900 had nineteen members, two more than did first Northwestern ensemble of 1898.

LIST OF UNIVERSITY GRID GREATS included Jesse Van Doozer and A. B. Potter, star backs in 1895.

increased with the construction, in 1891, on the present site of the men's quadrangles, of Sheppard Field, named for the University's business manager, Professor R. D. Sheppard. From the grandstand, which had a seating capacity of seven hundred, loyal supporters could wave the new purple and white colors (adopted in 1894), cheer as the great backs Van Doozer, Potter and Hunter plunged through the line, or chorus in derision after the decisive defeat of Chicago's giants in 1896:

"Team wanted; team wanted;
    That's the way the sign appeared
        above the door.
Team wanted; team wanted;
    That's the reason Stagg's so awful sore."

Despite its popularity, however, football had a precarious existence at Northwestern in the 1890's. Academic and athletic demands on the players' time were in continual conflict, and the Joint Athletic Committee, which controlled the teams, was continually pressed for

1890—FEATS OF EARLY FOOTBALL SQUAD enhanced interest of University students in new team sport.

money. In addition, the increasing savagery of football led President Rogers seriously to consider having the game abolished, although satisfactory regulations were adopted under the aegis of the newly formed Western Conference in 1896.

Baseball declined as football became the principal university sport, but Northwestern teams distinguished themselves in the Western Intercollegiate track meets held at Champaign and Chicago. Tennis became popular, especially after the victories in 1896 and 1897 of the women's team in the intercollegiate tournaments, and basketball was introduced among the ladies in 1898, although the men did not take it up until 1901.

After devoting himself to the interests of Northwestern for ten years, Dr. Rogers became convinced that the University might be advanced more rapidly under a new president. No satisfactory explanation for this decision has ever been published. In his report to the trustees for 1899-1900 Dr. Rogers asked for their support in his plan to increase the re-

CHAMPIONSHIP pole vault, executed by Northwestern track star. Track became popular sport during 1890's.

1895—FOOTBALL TEAM during practice in Sheppard Field. Walter Dill Scott was fifth from left in back.

STUDENTS USED TENNIS COURTS on Sheridan Road near Hatfield House. Early teams took many honors.

sources of the University by an appeal for $2,000,000 in donations. The President's challenge was not met, and on June 12, 1900, he resigned to become dean of the School of Law at Yale University.

Northwestern had progressed remarkably under Dr. Rogers' leadership. Both the assets of the University and the registration of stu-

dents had more than doubled. Outside the main organization of the University he had vigorously promoted the Alumni Association and the various committees for raising funds for Northwestern. The University entered the twentieth century with a well-knit organization, a prosperous financial condition and a confidence in future progress.

A Shifting Scene, 1900-1906

TREMONT HOUSE was home of professional schools.

Daniel Bonbright, the last of the "Old Faculty," succeeded Dr. Rogers as president ad interim. His short administration of two years, coming as it did between two regimes of brilliant progress, was necessarily a time for consolidation. The most important event during these two years was the purchase of the Tremont Hotel in Chicago for the grouping of the professional schools. In 1902, after considerable remodeling, the building was dedicated as the "Northwestern University Building," in which were housed the schools of Dentistry, Pharmacy and Law.

The chief problem of the time was the lack of living accommodations for the students, particularly for the men. Dr. Bonbright suggested that it might be necessary to limit the number of women students admitted, not

WILLARD HALL had addition constructed during 1890's to make room for large increase in coed enrollment.

only because their numbers were growing out of all proportion to those of the men, but also because of the dangers of "social distraction and dissipation, with their widening invasion of the serious purpose that should go with school life."

In January, 1902, Dr. Edmund Janes James was elected president of the University, and Dr. Bonbright resumed his duties as professor "with a gratifying sense of relief for an unwelcome duty well performed." Dr. James, a former student at Northwestern, was a man of brilliant mind and far-sighted vision. He had the assets of a great administrator— ability to delegate responsibility and understanding of all the departments of university activity. These qualities found almost immediate expression in Dr. James' support for the construction of men's dormitories, an adequate gymnasium and a student's union building. There was as yet no common meeting place for the men students on the campus, and "as a result they haunted the parlours of Willard Hall where the only touch of comfort or home atmosphere was to be found." Needless to say, this state of affairs was not at all welcome to the administration.

Hitherto building in the University had been done on a small scale, one structure being completed at a time. President James realized

that the funds of the University were not adequate to the fulfillment of his far-reaching plans and hence a campaign was launched to raise funds, particularly among the alumni, for the simultaneous construction of a new gymnasium, a commons, a social building, a new lecture building for the College of Liberal Arts and a chapel.

"It is clear," wrote the president, "that Northwestern University has passed in its financial operations from the list of small colleges into the category of great universities." President James recommended the sale of the unproductive property of the University to meet the deficits in the budget which had become almost chronic, and also the provision of one million dollars additional endowment to make possible future expansion. In 1903 Dr. Robert D. Sheppard resigned as business manager and treasurer and William A. Dyche, Arts '82, was elected as his successor. John R. Lindgren, Chicago banker and Northwestern trustee, was elected treasurer. In the same year the finances of the University were secured for a time from the attentions of the city tax authorities when the Illinois Supreme Court re-affirmed the 1879 court decision in favor of tax exemption of University property. Increasingly it was recognized that the University was serving a social function that

WILLIAM JENNINGS BRYAN spoke to audience of students and faculty during campus visit in 1903.

amply justified its tax privileges.

The rivalry of the new and progressive colleges of the Middle West was also forcing Northwestern to alter its curriculum. President James predicted that "in another twenty-five years no institution will rank as a university which does not make large provision for graduate work," and a bulletin was published during his first year of office, outlining a regular system of courses for obtaining graduate degrees. A number of fellowships and scholarships were established and the degree of Bachelor of Philosophy was abolished.

In 1902 it was announced that the University of Chicago was organizing a law school which was supposed to be the best in the West, and the South Side institution tried to entice a number of Northwestern's law faculty, including Dean Wigmore, to come to the new school. One member accepted the invitation. Thus challenged, Northwestern increased the income of its Law School by $10,000, established a full-time faculty of six professors and provided $20,000 for additions to the library and special equipment. The subjects of legal instruction were expanded and a revised curriculum for each of the three years of the course were adopted. Case-study methods were emphasized and the law library was augmented by twelve thousand volumes, through the generosity of Judge Elbert H. Gary, an alumnus of the school. In its early years the Law School had depended for its reputation largely on the individual fame of its faculty

JOHN H. WIGMORE was distinguished legal scholar.

JUDGE ELBERT H. GARY, long time chairman of Board of U. S. Steel, founded Gary, Indiana.

members. By the first decade of the twentieth century, however, the fame of its alumni was an increasing asset. In addition to Judge Gary, notable alumni included William Jennings Bryan, Judge Kenesaw Mountain Landis, Judge Harry Olson, Mrs. Catherine Waugh McCulloch and no less than four state governors, including Frank O. Lowden of Illinois.

President James had declared that in addition to giving instruction to students, every university ought to make some specific contribution to the general educational interests of the country. In the spirit of this declaration Northwestern sponsored two national educational conferences during the year 1903. On May 7 and 8 a conference of delegates from American colleges and universities met in the Northwestern University Building in Chicago to consider for the first time in this way "The Relation of the Colleges to the Professional Schools." Whether the liberal arts college had a field of its own or was merely a preparatory department for the professional schools, and whether or not a bachelor's degree should be required for entrance to the professional schools were problems which were

becoming increasingly important to Northwestern. They were thoroughly discussed by educational leaders from the entire country and the decisions arrived at influenced university development for a generation. As a result of this meeting a National College Association was formed and a second meeting was recommended for the following year.

On October 30 and 31 another conference was held in Evanston on "The Problems of Secondary Education." It concerned itself primarily with the broader questions of general educational policy of interest to teachers and laymen alike. The meeting included a celebration in honor of Dr. Herbert F. Fisk's thirty years of service to Northwestern, and served as forerunner to many similar conferences.

Many distinguished visitors came to the campus during President James' regime. Among the speakers at the inaugural ceremonies in 1902, for example, were Mr. Justice Oliver Wendell Holmes, who was making his first visit to the Middle West, Dr. Adolph Lorenz, noted Viennese surgeon, Dr. Alfred Nercincx of the University of Louvain, President William Rainey Harper of the University of Chicago

JUDGE KENESAW LANDIS, later national baseball commissioner, was famous alumnus of N.U. Law School.

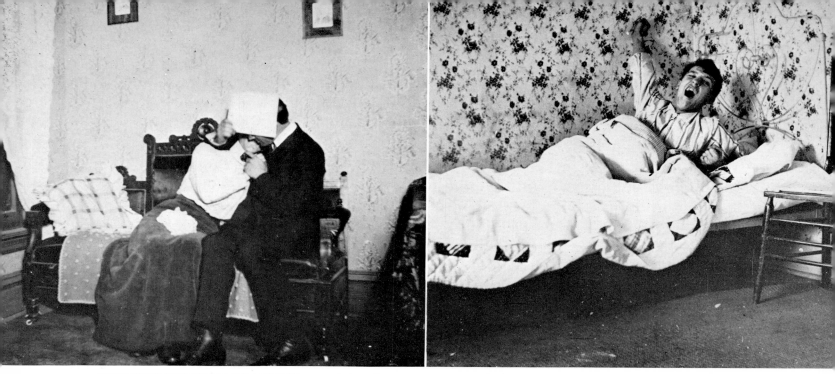

INQUIRING PHOTOGRAPHER recorded problems of Gay Nineties. Lack of privacy for romantic couples was a sociological problem. Copy of

doctoral dissertation protected incognitoes. Late rising and early lectures presented serious academic problems. Serious esthetic problem was the college string trio.

IMPROMPTU BAND created noisy rhythm on drum, dishpan, guitar, mandolin, and piano, to accompany hummers.

Portrait galleries and finely-constructed fraternity house furniture reflected standard of taste of decade. This was period when Beloit College was one of school's chief football rivals.

SQUIRRELS HAVE LIVED in campus oaks for generations, playfully begging nuts from coeds, professors, and citizens.

Student Life at Century's Turn

FRATERNITY STAG brought boys in nightshirts for an evening of horseplay.

1903—CROWDS CHEERED President Theodore Roosevelt when he returned to campus after 10 year interval.

and Dean Frederick Parker Walton of McGill University Law School. A notable event of President James' administration was the visit of President Theodore Roosevelt to the University campus in April, 1903. A mass parade conducted him through the town, where "the military band sent from Fort Sheridan struck up a lively tune and some of the citizens, somewhat precariously mounted on horseback, performed evolutions not in the program." The President inspected the campus, posed for his photograph on the steps of the Library and, in typically vigorous style, expressed his approval of higher education.

A former president of the University, in referring to his relationship with the board of trustees, remarked that, "It is my business to load this craft down to the gunwales. It is the business of the trustees to see that she does not sink." At the end of his report for 1904, President James recommended that provision be made for a "great graduate school" for the professional training of teachers, a school of technology for the training of engineers and a college of commerce and industry for the preparation of men of business. He pointed out that one million dollars would be

needed for the endowment of the College of Liberal Arts, $2,000,000 for a graduate school, $2,000,000 for a school of technology and $1,000,000 for the professional schools.

JAMES A. PATTEN, prominent member of Chicago Board of Trade, was trustee and generous donor to N.U.

The board of trustees, responsible as they were for the financial security of the University, may be forgiven for hesitating. The men who pulled the oars feared this program might wash over the gunwales. A conflict of aims thus developed between the ambitious president and the more cautious trustees which threatened the harmonious administration of the University. Suddenly, in the summer of 1904, Dr. James resigned to accept the presidency of the University of Illinois. The unexpected resignation was a relief of tension but also a blow to the University, for Dr. James had "set the University on a hill where it could be seen."

Dean Thomas Franklin Holgate of the College of Liberal Arts succeeded as president ad interim. The crisis in the affairs of the institution made his task a difficult one, but his two years' administration was one of steady, if unspectacular, progress and many of the plans of his predecessor were brought to fulfillment. An increase in endowment, advocated by President James, was planned by the board of trustees in a campaign to commemorate the fiftieth anniversary of the opening of the University. Under the leadership of James A. Patten, prominent Chicago business man, the drive secured one million dollars. Notable contributors, in addition to Mr. Patten, were Edward F. Swift, Norman Wait Harris (who endowed a series of public lectures on original research problems), Milton H. Wilson and William Deering. The result, in the words of President Holgate, was such that "the confidence felt by the increased strength will be felt in all the work of the university."

This confidence was only gradually translated into action. The need for a graduate school was still one of the chief topics of discussion among the members of the Liberal Arts faculty and President Holgate made a strong appeal to the trustees, pointing out that as long as the University's great scholars and investigators were forced to devote a large

EDWARD F. SWIFT, prominent Chicago meat packer who generously aided old School of Engineering.

NORMAN WAIT HARRIS contributed funds for Social Science building. Major part of Evanston campus is named in honor of Milton H. Wilson, trustee for many years. William Deering, supported school.

Thomas Franklin Holgate
Acting President
1904-1906 and 1916-1919

William A. Dyche
Business Manager
1902-1934

Fund, and periodical leaves of absence were instituted to give faculty members the opportunity to study abroad.

In 1905 the Medical School was brought under the complete control of the University, although the Women's Medical College, which had been short of funds during its thirty-two years of existence, lost its affiliation with the University in 1902. The affairs of the Law School were highlighted by the publication of Dean Wigmore's work on evidence, "the most complete and exhaustive treatise on a single branch of our law that has ever been written," according to the *Harvard Law Review*. An additional gift of more than five hundred volumes was made to the law library by Judge Gary and in 1906 the first number of the *Illinois Law Review* was published by members of the law faculty under the editorship of Professor Frederic C. Woodward. The Dental School gained additional prestige by increasing the requirement for the admission of students to graduation from an accredited high school, or the equivalent, and by increasing to three academic years the length of the course of study. At the same time the School of Music introduced one of the first courses in public school music methods to be offered in an American university.

Occasions for Northwestern to give useful service to the community began to multiply.

proportion of their time to undergraduate instruction the graduate school could not hope to develop. Lack of money also prevented such desirable advances as the enlargement of the scientific departments, and better provision for the physical welfare of students, including dormitories, dining hall and a gymnasium.

One improvement was made in 1905 when the finances of the College of Liberal Arts, which had hitherto functioned under a cloud of deficit, were systematized and adjusted to those of the other schools. In addition, a system of pensions for retiring members of the faculty was organized after Northwestern failed to qualify for the Carnegie Retirement

WOMAN'S MEDICAL SCHOOL did courageous pioneering work in education for women in Chicago.

MEDICAL SCHOOL had its headquarters at Dearborn and 25th in Chicago during years between 1893 and 1926.

At the Louisiana Purchase Exposition in St. Louis in 1904 Professor Henry S. White was chairman of the mathematics section, Professor Henry Crew chairman of the physics section and Dean Lutkin was the conductor of the Evanston Musical Club which triumphed in the Choral Contest. Further afield, Professor Arne Oldberg was honored by the American Music Society, his compositions being performed before the Twentieth Century Club in Boston. Dean Greene Vardiman Black delivered a series of lectures to the American Dental Society of Germany. Professor James A. James, in May, 1904, gave a course of lectures before the History Seminar of the Johns Hopkins University on French-American Diplomatic Relations, 1783-1801. In 1906, under the auspices of the National Civic Federation, Professor John H. Gray undertook the investigation of municipal ownership of public utilities in a number of cities in the United States.

Campus life during the early 1900's was, as usual, colorful. The past was remembered when the Class of 1905 donated a gun from

LAW LIBRARY, supported by Judge E. H. Gary, guided by Dean J. H. Wigmore, gathered noteworthy collections.

GERMAN SCHOLARS visited Evanston campus, discussed problems of language and teaching of German.

Fort Wadsworth to the University as a memorial to Northwestern's participation in the Civil War and the more recent past became history with the resignation of Northwestern's generous benefactor, William Deering, as president of the board of trustees. Jane Addams, Walter Wellman and Jacob Riis were featured speakers at meetings of the University Guild. On the lighter side the Bohemian Club, with its motto, "Pleasure is All and All is Pleasure," survived for one scintillating season, and a student was dismissed from the University for marrying while still an undergraduate.

In 1903, the *Northwestern* claimed the status of a daily for the first time with three issues a week. University activities were reported to the alumni through the *Northwestern University Alumni News Letter* and a "literary and alumni" journal, the *Northwestern Magazine*, had a brief and brilliant existence in 1904.

The expansive Mr. O'Flaherty extended his hospitality to students at 'O's Gem Lunch Room' and Dr. A. W. Patten, at morning chapel, noted wearily that, "Students have spent $150 on Y.M.C.A., $100 on foreign

ARNE OLDBERG was beloved professor of piano.

missions and $6,000 on formal parties. Let us pray."

Athletics continued to play a major role in student activities. A new board of control and an athletic association were formed and a women's grass hockey team was organized. The new football coach, Walter McCornack, produced a team which achieved third place in the Conference in 1903, and in 1905 a new athletic field on Central Street, with a grandstand seating capacity of 9,000, was dedicated. It was described in the press as "a field which, judged from its size, equipment, location and transportation facilities, is second to none in the United States."

At the same time, however, the future of football at Northwestern was seriously threatened. Despite reforms in the rules of the game, there was a continual toll of injuries and deaths throughout the country. At the end of 1905, moreover, the student-faculty Athletic Association, which had been reorganized in 1903 under the chairmanship of Professor

PROFESSOR JOHN H. GRAY investigated problems of municipal ownership of public utilities in U.S.

SOUTH CAMPUS was peaceful among its trees and around the 1905 class gift-memorial to students in Civil War.

Floyd Long, was hopelessly in debt and could no longer sponsor athletics. The board of trustees therefore decreed that all athletics were to become the responsibility of the University, under a director, and at the same time, in order to give sufficient time "for the development of more healthy conditions under which the game might be played," football should be discontinued as an intercollegiate sport for five years. Though this ban continued for only two years, it was most unpopular with the students, for it destroyed Northwestern's chances of distinction in the Conference for almost a decade.

EARLY SEASON GAME on new field. Increased injuries caused abolition of football at N.U. in 1906.

The Harris Regime, 1906-1916

In February, 1906, Dr. Holgate's administration came to an end with the election of Dr. Abram W. Harris as president. The new president came with a background of varied experience in the organization of the University of Maine and of the Jacob Tome Institute in Maryland. His best talents were needed, for Northwestern had begun expansion in a spirit of optimism and the prosperity of the University was threatened by the financial depression of 1906-07.

LARGE CROWDS GATHERED in wooden stands on Central Street for football games in early years of century.

Abram W. Harris
President, 1906-1916

CAMPUS MEADOW ceased to serve as pasture, was surrounded by buildings.

The national economic situation has been, to a large extent, the index of Northwestern's fortunes. The financial history of the University has been one of alternation between periods of prosperity, during which expansion has been undertaken or planned, and periods of depression, in which donations have almost ceased, expansion has been postponed and even the vision of a greater university has sometimes been lost from view. Until the beginning of the twentieth century hard times meant a threat to the existence of the institution. After 1900, however, this existence was never seriously threatened.

Measures taken to combat adversity during President Harris' regime illustrate this new security. Despite the curtailment of building plans, the postponement of salary increases and a burden of deficit which plagued University budgets up until the outbreak of the World War in 1914, there was a slight expansion even during depression years. Stopgap donations by trustees and alumni helped to minimize the threat of deficits while efforts were made to secure new endowment and economies were effected through reorganization of the budget. In 1908 a decision of the Illinois Supreme Court finally removed the threat of taxation of University property. A number of substantial gifts were made during the early years of the Harris administration, and the Alumni Endowment Fund, founded by the graduating class in 1907, was especially active in supporting the construction of the new gymnasium.

Not only did the University lack an ade-

quate auditorium for large gatherings such as commencement, but the original gymnasium, in William Hard's words, "was born old," and a quarter of a century of use had not improved it much. The construction of a modern

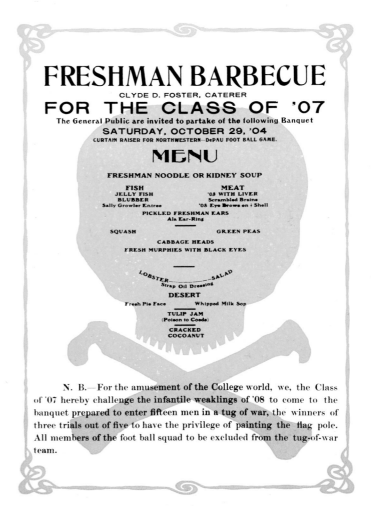

FRESHMAN BARBECUE
CLYDE D. FOSTER, CATERER
FOR THE CLASS OF '07
The General Public are invited to partake of the following Banquet
SATURDAY, OCTOBER 29, '04
CURTAIN RAISER FOR NORTHWESTERN—DePAU FOOT BALL GAME.
MENU

FRESHMAN NOODLE OR KIDNEY SOUP

FISH   MEAT
JELLY FISH   '08 WITH LIVER
BLUBBER   Scrambled Brains
Sally Growler Entree   '08 Eye Brows on ½ Shell

PICKLED FRESHMAN EARS
Ala Ear-Ring

SQUASH   GREEN PEAS

CABBAGE HEADS
FRESH MURPHIES WITH BLACK EYES

LOBSTER——————SALAD
Strap Oil Dressing

DESERT

Fresh Pie Face   Whipped Milk Sop

TULIP JAM
(Poison to Coeds)

CRACKED
COCOANUT

N. B.—For the amusement of the College world, we, the Class of '07 hereby challenge the infantile weaklings of '08 to come to the banquet prepared to enter fifteen men in a tug of war, the winners of three trials out of five to have the privilege of painting the flag pole. All members of the foot ball squad to be excluded from the tug-of-war team.

CLASS RIVALRIES were strong in 1904 when sophomore's posted this banquet menu of freshman delicacies.

PATTEN GYMNASIUM stood on present site of Technological Institute. Famous statutes now adorn new Patten.

building, however, presented an almost impossible problem of financing, until one day in the summer of 1908, when Dr. Harris went to lunch with a "friend" and came away with the promise of $150,000 for the new building from James A. Patten. The gymnasium included a large indoor athletic field (forerunner of modern college field houses), a club room for men, offices for instructors, an extensive swimming pool, and a gymnasium room with a seating capacity of 1,200. The building immediately became the center of intercollegiate field sports in the Middle West. It provided the pattern on which many other university gymnasiums were built, and until it was razed in 1940 to make way for the Technological Institute, remained the most notable architectural structure on the Evanston campus.

The commencement exercises of 1909 were memorable: the present good fortune of the University was acknowledged by holding the ceremonies in the new gymnasium, and the past was recognized by the award of the B.A. degree (as of the class of 1862) to Edward Spencer, hero of the wreck of the *Lady Elgin* in 1860. Spencer was present in a wheelchair. The pattern of commencements changed again in the following year when the custom was introduced of having four students from the grad-

EDWARD SPENCER of *Lady Elgin* fame received degree 49 years later.

OLD PATTEN GYM served as center of indoor sports, intercollegiate competitions and public gatherings.

uating class give commencement addresses. Scholastic distinction was encouraged by making public mention of students with the highest scholastic standing in each class. Special honors were awarded, including the Orrington Lunt Essay Prize, the Harris Prize in political and social science, and by 1914, also, the Daniel Bonbright Scholarship in literary studies and the Oliver Marcy Scholarship in science.

The Music School profited greatly from the construction of the new gymnasium. Dean Lutkin organized a Chicago North Shore Festival Association which held a musical festival in the gymnasium in the first week of June, 1909, featuring performances by Madame Schumann-Heink and David Bispham, and a chorus of 600 voices. Dr. Lutkin had already organized the famous A Cappella Choir in 1906 and in 1909 facilities were further enlarged with the installation of a pipe organ in Fisk Chapel. From the small beginnings in 1891 of a director and four instructors within the College of Liberal Arts, the School of Music grew by 1913 to a fully equipped and successful organization of thirty-two faculty members and an enrollment of 567.

A further step was taken toward the establishment of a graduate school when in 1910 the Committee on Graduate Studies was transformed into the Board of Graduate Studies. Of the twenty-one faculty members on the new board, fifteen were from the College of Liberal Arts, three from the Medical School, two from the Law School and one from the College of Engineering. In 1917 this board was reconstituted as the Graduate School, and that same year Northwestern gained prestige by election as a member of the Association of American Universities. James A. James, who had been chairman of the graduate board since 1913, became the first dean of the Graduate School.

In 1905 the Medical School, living up to its reputation for leadership, became the first school in the country to recognize the standing of nurses by granting them diplomas, and in 1909 the Evanston Hospital Association Training School for Nurses was affiliated with Northwestern. In 1908 the Medical School entrance requirements were increased to a

COAST GUARD STATION provided valuable extracurricular activity, and helped to save many lives.

UNIVERSITY SYMPHONY orchestra played in Patten Gym, from beginning received critics' praise.

UNIVERSITY ALUMNI gathered then as later to get reacquainted and to discuss "the good old days."

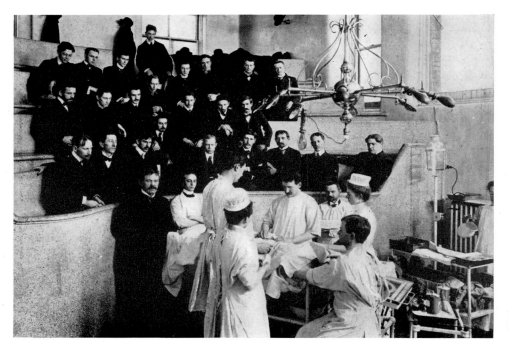

JOHN H. LONG dean of School of Pharmacy,
member of National Pure Food Commission.

minimum of one year of university work and in 1911 this minimum was raised to two years. There were also large increases in the resources of the School. James A. Patten contributed $250,000 toward its endowment and James Deering $1,000,000 to be devoted to the charity work of Wesley Hospital as an aid to the clinical work of the School. Laboratory facilities were augmented with the completion of the University Dispensary at Mercy Hospital and by the donation of a tuberculosis research laboratory by Mr. Patten. For a number of years the School had pub-

lished a *Bulletin* of its activities and in 1909 this was expanded into *The Medical Journal*, a quarterly for the publication of important discoveries made by the faculty and by alumni. The School of Pharmacy, which marked its silver jubilee in 1911, began a policy of closer integration with the Medical School, largely on the initiative of the new dean, Dr. John H. Long. Dr. Long also brought prestige to Northwestern through his work on the National Pure Food Commission in 1908.

Fifty years of achievement were commemorated by the Law School in 1909 with the sponsoring of a national conference on Criminal Law and Criminology, the first such conference to be held in the United States. This was also the first large-scale attempt to apply the results of research in criminology to the science of criminal procedure and it resulted in the organization of the American Institute of Criminal Law and Criminology, of which Dean Wigmore was the first president.

In 1905 a dental clinic was added to the School of Dentistry and an experimental postgraduate course, begun in 1906, was placed on a permanent basis. Perhaps the most important step taken in the Dental School during the early years of the twentieth century, however, was the introduction of the lecture-recitation method in 1915-16. This quiz section approach, already adopted in many of

GREENE VARDIMAN BLACK'S office contained equipment which was typical of best dentistry of day.

WILLARD E. HOTCHKISS saw opportunities for evening study, was first dean of Commerce School.

JOSEPH SCHAFF-NER was interested in School of Commerce.

the other schools, enabled the Dental School to offer a far wider range of courses and made necessary an expansion of its facilities, in particular the provision of a museum and a library which has become the most extensive of its kind in the world.

Under President Harris' administration two new schools were added to Northwestern and a third more closely affiliated. Willard E. Hotchkiss, who became a member of the economics department in 1905, saw the need and opportunity for an evening school of commerce, offering courses in business to the young men and women employed in Chicago. With the cooperation and counsel of Joseph Schaffner, a public-spirited Chicago business-man, the support and financial backing of the Chicago Association of Commerce, the Illinois Society of Certified Public Accountants and the Chicago Industrial Club were obtained and the establishment of the School made possible.

The first class opened in the fall of 1907 under Professor Earl Dean Howard with some thirty-five students, including a considerable number who later became well known in Chicago business. The new School formally opened in the fall of 1908 with Willard Hotchkiss as its first dean. Under his leadership the School

Arthur Andersen was student, teacher, trustee.

Alfred Bays was both professor and trustee.

proved its worth and became so popular that within a few years it had grown to be one of the largest in the University. Included in the faculty lists during the early years were the names of a number of individuals who later became identified with the growth and development of the University as a whole, such as Walter Dill Scott, Homer Vanderblue, Arthur Andersen, Alfred Bays and Arthur Swanson.

President James, in his inaugural address in 1902, had declared, in reference to the influence of technical courses on the study of the humanities: "The very emphasis which pure and applied science has received in our modern educational system by the union of the technical school and the university has made its contribution to the revolution in the study of the humanities which has marked the last generation in this country." Unfortunately a lack of funds had retarded the development of technical studies at Northwestern, but the erection of Swift Hall of Engineering, the gift of Mrs. Gustavus Swift and her son, Edward F. Swift, in 1909, made possible the organization of a distinct College of Engineering with separate facilities in the five-year course of study for cultural as well as technical subjects. It was a new departure in university organization designed, as the new director, Dr. John F. Hayford, pointed out, to ensure that all students of the College received a well-rounded, rather than merely a mechanical education.

In 1915 Director Cumnock of the School of Oratory requested that the School become an integral part of the University. Entrance requirements were coordinated with those of the College of Liberal Arts and the academic year of the school was lengthened to thirty-six weeks. In 1916 Director Cumnock retired, ending nearly half a century of service to the University, and was succeeded by Ralph B. Dennis.

The total scene was varied and colorful. It was the age of the telephone and rural free delivery, when optimistic progress was still the keynote of the times, and coeds observed

EARLY BUSINESS OFFICE of University stood between business establishments in downtown Evanston.

1909—SWIFT HALL of Engineering was opened to provide needed facilities for students of technology.

ORRINGTON LUNT LIBRARY made space for 100,000 books, pleasant contrast with old study rooms in U.H.

that "an up-to-date girl is not fitted to be the heroine of a novel . . . her mannish shoes incapacitate her for pacing the boudoir." Franklyn Bliss Snyder revealed the beauties of Burns' poetry to his classes in English literature, A. C. L. Brown became professor of English and Arthur Guy Terry became an instructor in history.

In 1911 a $40,000 heating plant was added to the University and green caps were made compulsory for freshmen. Under the direction of the new librarian, Dr. Walter Lichtenstein, Lunt Library expanded to 100,000 volumes, demonstrating the inadequacy of the library building to accommodate future increases. An important need was met in 1915 when a separate department of political science was organized under the chairmanship of Norman Dwight Harris. Wendell David became the first Rhodes Scholar from Illinois and Dr. Bonbright died in 1912 after fifty-four years of teaching at Northwestern. In the same year Glenn Frank became the first secretary of the Alumni Association. The girls of Chapin Hall received the censure of Dean Mary Potter for "dancing on the oiled floor of the library," and the riotous celebration of the Annual Northwestern Circus evolved out of the staid beginnings of a Y. M. C. A. County Fair.

MARY ROSS POTTER was rated strict but fair as dean of women.

The new increases in the facilities of Northwestern required a reorganization of administration. The University Council was reconstituted with A. H. Wilde, the University historian, as Secretary in charge of University publicity. A Campus Commission was appointed in 1909 and drew up a plan for two campuses in Evanston—the north, or "residence" campus and the south, or "official" campus. The present semi-circular arrangement of buildings from Lunt Library southward was adopted and a new library on the

STUDENTS TAKE TIME OUT from picnic fun to show off pointed shoes and bonnets.

STAFF OF DAILY NORTHWESTERN worked hard preparing issue.

HEATING PLANT WORKER, E. O. Smith, enjoyed moments of relaxation with catnaps in rocker.

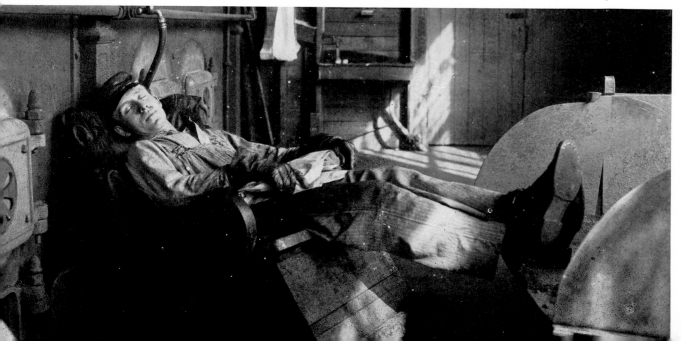

1914—MAY QUEEN AND COURT, amid flowers, posed before traditional ceremonies.

STUDENTS showed class spirit with gaudy identifying finery.

GIRLS IN GYM CLASSES dressed in traditional uniform.

GRADUATION CEREMONIES, as usual, brought families back together, presaged separation of classmates.

WINTER WEATHER permitted hockey on North Campus.

FROSH-SOPH pole greased for annual scrap.

SOCCER GAMES were sometimes serious, but sometimes burlesqued with high silk hats, skirts, and waiters.

WELL-DRESSED COEDS
grouped by Fisk Academy.

1914—STUDENTS MOVED into first
of North Quadrangle fraternity houses.

A. H. WILDE, history professor, first secretary of University Council.

SIGMA CHI house, typical of pre-quadrangle period.

site of Heck Hall was contemplated, a plan that was considerably advanced by the destruction of Heck Hall by fire in February, 1914. New plans, made as a result of this event, also included the acquisition of Memorial Hall from Garrett Biblical Institute within seven years. The College of Liberal Arts was finally able to expand from its cramped quarters in the older buildings with the completion, in December, 1915, of Harris Hall, a classic structure of Indiana limestone, embodying the finest constructional techniques of the time. The building was the gift of Norman Wait Harris, a trustee of the University and one of its most generous patrons.

Meanwhile the north campus was develop-

ing. By 1914 seven fraternity chapter houses and four dormitories had been completed. Three of the dormitories were named in memory of former presidents Hinman, Foster and Haven, while the fourth was named for John R. Lindgren, the donor and the University's treasurer. By a farsighted building policy Northwestern avoided the scandal of mortgage-plastered mansions built by fraternities and prevented the undemocratic influences which such unrestricted development created. Fraternity and non-fraternity students thereafter lived together in the same quadrangle, although in separate houses. The fraternities built their houses, under control as to style and extent, on money advanced in part by

ONE SECTION of North Quadrangles, which included seven fraternity houses, four open dormitories.

FIREMAN WORKED VALIANTLY with the best of engines but could not prevent Heck Hall destruction.

FEBRUARY COLD made salvage of personal belongings extremely difficult on day after fire.

Fire Destroyed
Heck Hall

WHEN FIRE gutted Heck Hall in February 1914, students were on vacation. Site was used for Deering Library.

WATER FROZE on windows, railings, and ledges as firemen attempted to halt blaze.

COEDS SOLD SANDWICHES to obtain funds for student union building even before World War I.

the University. This was to be paid back within forty years, after which time the University would charge a dollar a year rental and continue to own and control the sites. Similar conditions were established for the sororities when the Women's Campus was developed during the 1920's.

May 26, 1916, was designated as Northwestern Night and alumni meetings were held in centers throughout the country. Messages were read from alumni in distant places and the first of the famous candle-lighting ceremonies was held. A purple candle more than four feet high and six inches thick was placed in the tower of Old College by Horace Goodrich, a graduate of the class of 1859 and son of one of the founders. The candle was lighted for fifteen minutes annually on Founders' Day, January 28, in commemoration of the successful establishment of the University, and alumni groups throughout the world began to hold ceremonies using a common ritual.

President Harris resigned in the summer of 1916 and Dean Holgate once more became acting president. This second administration of Dean Holgate had scarcely begun when war forced a reorientation of academic life. Nevertheless some sound reorganization was achieved, particularly in the revision of the University's statutes and the creation of a Board of Admissions.

The future was also foreshadowed with the suggestion, early in 1917, that the Chicago schools be moved to a common site on the North Side of Chicago and that building plans be prepared. The idea was, in part, that of Dean Wigmore, but the grand scheme of a complete campus on the North Side was the work of General Nathan William MacChesney. A committee of the board of trustees was appointed to consider the proposal but the war forced an indefinite delay.

President Wilson no longer called upon his countrymen to be neutral, even in thought, as the cloud of war which had hung so long over America broke early in 1917. Some of Northwestern's sons had long since ceased to be neutral. While B. S. Hutchinson, Med. '06, of the Canadian Expeditionary Force, won the Victoria Cross, Albert Jaster of the Dental School received the Iron Cross from Germany's "All Highest", and Professor Philip Fox of the astronomy department anticipated his country's participation by several months and began teaching courses in military training and organization. The Medical School set up a course in military training for its students, and from this school came Northwestern's first substantial contribution to the war effort.

The appeal of the Allies for hospital facilities was responded to early in May, 1917, with the formation of the famous Northwestern medical corps, Hospital Unit No. 12, under Dr. Frederick A. Besely. Financed in part by the University, it cared for more than 60,000 Allied wounded during the last two years of the war. More than three hundred Northwesterners took part in its activities and six died while with the unit.

At the time of the American declaration of war it was generally believed that the

1917—PRESIDENT WILSON addressed joint session of Congress, asked for and received declaration of war.

fighting would soon be over. Many Northwestern students joined ambulance units and some went in with Sherwood Eddy's Y.M.C.A. unit for the quickest service overseas. The Y.M.C.A. unit, with strong financial support from the University, did good work in France, and later most of the members transferred into the armed forces. Many of those who joined the ambulance units found themselves doing non-combatant duty in Camp Chillicothe, while their less impulsive classmates were going overseas in fighting units.

Before the end of the spring semester 350 students left for active service. The faculty decided that those who enlisted before the term's end should be given credit for the full term, but at the same time there was an appeal, reenforced by General Leonard Wood, for students to remain in school until called under the Selective Service Act. The academic year was also reorganized at this time on a quarter system, in order to speed up the education of those eligible for the draft.

Professor Fox went away to join the regular army and President Holgate, anxious that Northwestern take part in the war effort to fullest extent, secured the services of Lieutenant W. W. Lang, a physically disabled Canadian officer, as instructor to the rapidly mobilized University training corps. During the fall term, with what arms and equipment could be obtained, "Lang's Army," five hundred strong, marched along the lake front, prepared to undertake the defense of the campus or the more modest task of clearing the snow from Evanston streets after the record snowfall of January, 1918. By spring, the president had obtained a regular R.O.T.C. officer, Lieutenant Losie J. Williams, and equipment such as uniforms and condemned Russian rifles.

The University also mobilized 800 women students in National Aid and Red Cross work,

Y.M.C.A. gathered large numbers of young men for annual banquet in spacious Patten Gymnasium.

DEEP SNOW of 1918 piled high at Sheridan Road and University Place, long remembered by S.A.T.C. shovelers.

under the direction of Dean Mary Ross Potter. The girls were enrolled in courses in food and fuel conservation, principles of agriculture and first aid, all designed to augment the all-out war work of the nation. War bond drives (Northwestern as a whole subscribed nearly $100,000 to the Third Liberty Loan), student government, editing the *Daily Northwestern* and land army activities on the University's farm at Libertyville were also undertaken.

The organization of the University itself had to be adjusted to meet the new demands of war. The School of Pharmacy was transferred to the control of the University of Illinois and the Academy was discontinued since it had now outlived its need and proved a drain on resources needed elsewhere. War work was coordinated under a Northwestern University War Council, and a committee of faculty and alumni was formed to cooperate with the National Research Council in providing skilled leadership for the war effort.

It was in this phase of its war activities that Northwestern achieved marked distinction. In a short time the faculty was depleted through extensive volunteering for war service. Dean John F. Hayford of the College of Engineering became an adviser to the National Board on Aeronautics and Dean John H. Wigmore a member of the Judge Advocate General's Staff. Professor W. Lee Lewis of the chemistry department devised "Lewisite" gas to destroy the enemy with increased efficiency. Dr. Walter Dill Scott, later Colonel, offered his services to the War Department for assisting in the implementation of the Selective Service Act. Here he evolved his

COLONEL WALTER DILL SCOTT planned personnel tests and officer candidate program.

98

FRENCH BOX CARS of 40 men and 8 horses variety provided transportation for doughboys.

FLAG WAVING BEAUTY assisted recruiting officers to obtain volunteers from Northwestern.

CANADIAN MEDICAL corps loaded wounded on ambulance. Students joined units before U.S. entry.

ENLIST HERE NOW
First Illinois Infantry

ASTRONOMER'S HOME was headquarters of S.A. T.C. Wooden barracks in background housed the unit.

famous methods for the selection of drafted personnel for the most suitable occupations in the forces and for the selection of officer material according to efficiency ratings.

Further afield Northwestern was also active. Colonel Abel Davis, an alumnus of the Law School, took the 132nd Infantry Regiment into action in the Argonne and General Nathan W. MacChesney served on the Judge Advocate General's Staff in France. Dean Ralph Dennis of the School of Speech, after an amazing series of adventures as a Y.M.C.A. worker in Russia, found himself as American vice-consul in Moscow, and Franklin Bellows and David Hanson left distinguished names on the honor roll of American war dead.

On the campus the war effort underwent some significant changes. Drafted men, in varying numbers, were assigned to the Northwestern campus to be taught technical trades and both teaching staff and campus buildings were made available to them. In addition, the National Committee on Education and Special Training proposed that all university campuses should become training centers to prevent the wastage of colleges through in-

REVIEWING S.A.T.C.— Lt. Williams, General Barry, President Holgate, General MacChesney.

GENERAL MacCHESNEY addressed first parade of Northwestern's S.A.T.C. Unit on October 1, 1918.

discriminate volunteering, a proposal that resulted in the formation of the short-lived Student Army Training Corps. Under its authority all men of military age in college lived and worked under army discipline and regulations. Fraternity houses and dormitories became barracks, and regular barracks and a mess hall were built on the campus. In addition to the unpopular S.A.T.C. a more exclusive Naval S.A.T.C. was also formed on the campus and billeted in Garrett Biblical Institute. The first burst of enthusiasm for the war had been replaced by an atmosphere of deadly frustration and monotony, broken

STUDENTS' ARMY TRAINING CORPS numbered thirteen hundred volunteers before Armistice Day.

only by the more horrible relief of the influenza epidemic of 1918.

These hazards of the home front at war did not last long. On November 11 Marshal Foch received the German plenipotentiaries in the forest of Compiègne, and a snake dance of Northwestern students through the streets of Evanston proclaimed that the "War to End Wars" was over. Northwestern, in common with the rest of the Allied world, was soon concerned with counting the cost of the war and solving the problems of demobilization. Northwestern's sons and daughters to the number of 3606 had gone to the war and 65, remembered in 1923 in the planting of the Avenue of Elms, had lost their lives.

During time of crisis the public duty of a university becomes especially obvious and Northwestern moved unhesitatingly to fulfill her obligation to the nation. Thus it was that the war partly changed, partly only dramatized the function of the University in the community. For no university exists merely to educate individuals in special subjects. Its purpose goes far beyond that and requires it to serve society by teaching, research and direct participation.

Demobilization was accomplished swiftly. The S.A.T.C., bane of students and faculty alike, disappeared within a month. Other

Lynn Harold Hough
President
1919-1920

problems of the war period could not be so lightly dismissed. Strained financial resources had to be bolstered and readjustments had to be made among the faculty as a result of temporary and permanent vacancies. The needs of the University in the matter of endowment were greater than ever.

The new developments were to be undertaken under a new administration, however, for in May, 1919, Dr. Lynn Harold Hough succeeded Dr. Holgate as president of the University. In addition to the burdens of administration during the war years, Dr. Hol-

1916—PATRIOTIC NOTE was expressed in May Day Festival with Miss Columbia and other colorful figures.

gate had been active in national educational affairs, in outside war work and in supporting the movement in favor of the League of Nations. He had been a devoted servant of the University, undertaking a thankless and difficult duty with courage and determination at a time of great emergency.

Dr. Hough's one-year administration was brief, but it came in that post-war dawn when dreams were being born. Something of the future was already envisioned and first steps were taken toward realization. Financial assistance from national boards of the Methodist Church helped to bring a corps of instructors for a department of religious education and missions in the College of Liberal Arts and Graduate School, and a department of education was launched. In addition the School of Commerce, under its vigorous dean, Ralph Emerson Heilman, established a day division in 1919.

Finances were a fundamental issue. Dr. Holgate had called for $5,000,000 in endowment and Milton H. Wilson, in June, 1919, made a conditional gift of $172,000 with the purpose of helping to stabilize the budget.

A committee appointed to prepare a report on financial needs advised that a campaign be launched to obtain the colossal sum of $25,371,200 within ten years, of which $4,000,000 would be needed almost immediately. Another $1,500,000 would be needed within a year to purchase the site of the proposed Chicago North Side campus, at Chicago Avenue and the lake front. In support of this challenging program one-half million dollars was donated by Milton H. Wilson toward unrestricted endowment; other donors followed this example so that by the beginning of 1920 subscriptions amounted to $750,000. A University Campaign Committee was then appointed under the chairmanship of William A. Dyche and a drive for further contributions was carried on among the students and alumni which secured the promise of $300,000 more.

The chief center of interest was, of course, the new Chicago Campus, which presented an opportunity for expansion unprecedented in the University's history. Support for the purchase of the tract among the trustees was not unanimous, however. James A. Patten opposed it strenuously, as being beyond the University's means, and advocated the consolidation of the professional schools on the Evanston campus. Nevertheless the majority of the trustees favored the proposal and in June, 1920, the purchase was authorized.

The second period of growth and consolidation had come to an end, and the University was on the threshold of new ventures when Dr. Hough resigned on account of ill health. The middle period, 1890-1920, had seen the increasing influence of science on the university curriculum and the closer integration of the professional schools. The importance of research was emphasized both in the development of the Graduate School and in the altered character of the faculties. Men were chosen in this epoch increasingly for their capacity to carry on major research projects. But there was a dual emphasis, as there must be in a great university. Teaching was of fundamental significance, as well as the training of teachers and scholars. A continuing process of reform in curricula stressed broader education and higher standards.

Only part of the work of the university can be carried on within its walls. There must also be association with other academic and civic institutions if higher education and the community are to benefit. Development of Northwestern's role as part of the community and the nation was really begun in the 1890's and this role expanded steadily during the early years of the twentieth century. Educational and scientific conferences furnished occasions for comparison of academic achievement, and association with city, state and nation became closer. The service role of the University became more apparent both to the administration of Northwestern and to the leaders of the business world.

Changes were great and the disruptions which accompanied them were also great. There was often division of opinion on the line of development which the University was to follow. Yet the work of improvement went on, despite disagreement as to the means of accomplishing it, despite depressions and two wars. The University had passed from the era of insecure beginnings. It had gone through a period of development and testing. The next thirty years of its first century were to be characterized by energetic maturity. By 1920 the vision of a Greater Northwestern was clearly formulated.

LIFE SAVING CREW practiced special technique of Captain Lawson for righting boat in stormy waters.

THE GREATER
NORTHWESTERN
1920-1951

PATTEN GYMNASIUM

THE GREATER NORTHWESTERN

1920~1951

Walter Dill Scott, President, 1920-1939

IN choosing a successor for Dr. Hough in 1920, the board of trustees broke with tradition. First, the new president, unlike his predecessors in office, was an alumnus of the University. In addition, he was a Presbyterian, whereas previous presidents had been Methodists. Northwestern was ready in many ways to break new ground.

In the course of his address at President Walter Dill Scott's installation, Dr. Arthur A. Hammerschlag, president of Carnegie Institute of Technology, acknowledged the great advances which had been made in the natural and applied sciences, but declared: "What the country needs greatly, and little attention has been directed to it, is a study of personnel. . . . In the renaissance of higher education through which we are now passing the doctrine of the selection of the right men and women to re-interpret life is the most important question now confronting the educators of the world."

Franklyn Bliss Snyder, President, 1939-1949

The emphasis in a university curriculum changes with the changing needs of society. In the first forty years of Northwestern's development the primary emphasis had been on the humanities—the liberal curriculum that had been the ideal of higher education since the Renaissance. The second period, between 1890 and 1920, was marked by an emphasis upon professional and scientific studies in keeping with the technological nature of the age. The third period, beginning in 1920, placed a new emphasis on the social sciences. Men and women had to be trained to deal with the complex social problems of the modern era.

BUILDINGS ADDED during last 30 years include entire Chicago Campus, Deering Library, Technological Institute, new Patten Gym, Howes Chapel, Swift additions, and Scott Hall.

James Roscoe Miller, President, 1949—

GIRLS HAD FUN learning to be climbers in gymnasium class, dressed in bloomers which still shocked some.

A Decade of Vision, 1920-1930

It was symptomatic of the changed emphasis that, in his inaugural address, President Scott should describe Northwestern as a "service institution." "A university is neither buildings nor equipment, but the characters and minds of men and women. Its life and continuity are not in stone or timber or fine tools, but in productive process and creation. . . . The least conspicuous thing about this university is buildings. And the most conspicuous is the cooperation we are giving, and receiving from, all manifestations of culture and economics."

The first problem of the new administration dealt with finance. An increase in tuition fees was made for the purpose of increasing faculty salaries and attracting additional distinguished scholars. The principal stress, however, was placed upon securing a sound basis of permanent endowment on which to build the "Greater Northwestern." In 1922 a campaign was launched for $1,400,000 to meet the conditions of a $600,000 offer made by the General Education Board of New York for the purpose of increasing salaries of the faculty and staff. Under the chairmanship of Trustee Robert Campbell, the goal of the campaign was soon reached and then expanded to $5,100,000. This sum was required to cover immediate needs and expected deficits of all the schools and to make possible limited future expansion.

Times were prosperous, a general spirit of optimism pervaded the nation, and patrons of Northwestern were prepared to donate generously. Mark W. Cresap organized the board of trustees Committee on Publicity and the importance of Northwestern as a field for investment was popularized in a brilliantly successful campaign. By Commencement of 1923, $700,000 in subscriptions was forthcoming, of which over $200,000 had been secured by the students. Notable among the contributions were those of Judge Elbert Gary for the endowment of the Law Library, William Smith Mason for a chair of American history and Charles Deering for a chair of botany in the College of Liberal Arts. By the beginning of 1924 nearly eight and a half million dollars, sixty per cent more than the original objective, had been pledged.

The General Alumni Association was formed in 1921 through a consolidation of alumni associations of the various schools. Up to that time little systematic effort had been made to keep in touch with alumni after their departure from the University. Bishop George Craig Stewart was the first president and the *Northwestern University Alumni News* was established by the Association for keeping in touch with alumni and acquainting them with the activities of the University.

Meanwhile the facilities of the University were expanded and reorganized. The year 1921 saw the opening of the Medill School of Journalism in association with the School of Commerce. The *Chicago Tribune* and its editors, Colonel Robert R. McCormick and Captain Joseph Medill Patterson, pledged a fixed sum to underwrite the expenses of the School, which was named in memory of Joseph

MARK CRESAP organized board of trustees Committee on Publicity to increase University donations.

Medill, founder of the *Tribune*. In the same year the School of Oratory was changed in name to the School of Speech, and a four-year course for the degree of Bachelor of Letters was authorized. The creation of a Board of Supervision brought the heterogen-

READING AND REFERENCE ROOM of Gary Law School Library provided books at hand, quiet atmosphere.

eous student activities under one organization, and the Summer School was reconstructed and a director placed in charge. In 1924 a department of Women's Health was set up and in 1925 a similar department was provided for the men.

Shortly after the First World War Dean Arthur Black of the Dental School, son of Greene Vardiman Black, introduced a program of graduate and postgraduate courses on a very wide scale and added a department for dental hygienists to the Dental School. The graduate courses in dentistry comprised the first successful program of study on the graduate level in dentistry and set the pattern which was subsequently followed by other schools. Dr. Black also made a major contribution to dental research by organizing and successfully completing an index of the periodical literature from its beginning in 1839 which was continued by the American Dental Association.

Great fortunes of the Middle West were being directed into new channels of service to

CHICAGO WAS LABORATORY for students in study of law, commerce, and all problems of metropolitan life.

CHARLES H. DEERING, trustee and Northwestern benefactor. Deering Library was named in his memory.

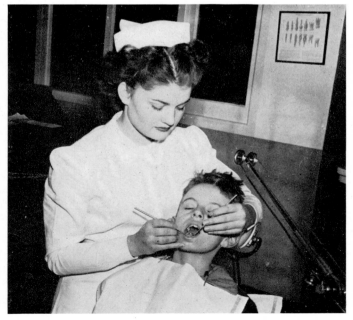

HYGIENISTS AND DOCTORS of Dental School helped save teeth of many boys and girls in Chicago.

110

MRS. MONTGOMERY WARD donated and endowed Montgomery Ward Memorial building on Chicago Campus.

the youth of both section and nation. The development of the Chicago Campus, principal object of the financial campaigns of the early 1920's, was representative of this trend. The various campaign committees were successful in interesting the general public in Northwestern, but it would have been impossible to complete the new campus without the substantial donations of a few benefactors who combined generosity with a vision of a great University.

Mrs. Montgomery Ward, widow of the builder of the famous mail order house, made the greatest contribution late in 1923. She gave more than four and a half million dollars for the construction of the 18-story Montgomery Ward Memorial Building, the medical-dental center of the University, and a further four million dollars was later given for the maintenance of the center. Mrs. George Thorne, sister of Mrs. Ward, donated $250,000 to erect the

WIEBOLDT HALL became handsome home of School of Commerce on Chicago Campus, served also University College.

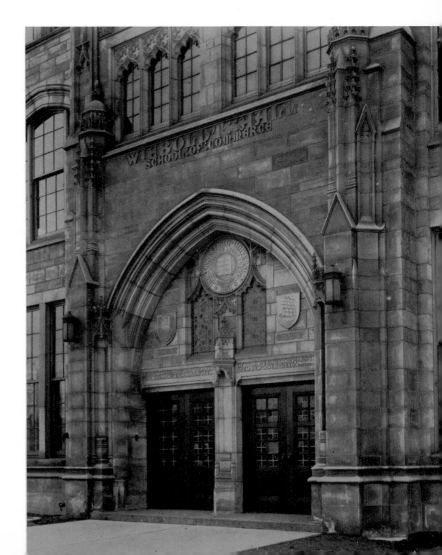

NORTHWESTERN EPOCH—ground breaking, Mrs. Levy Mayer, Mrs. George Thorne, Mrs. Montgomery Ward, President Scott, Mrs. and Mr. George McKinlock, Mrs. and Mr. Werner Wieboldt, Judge Elbert Gary.

LINCOLN HALL in Levy Mayer Law School building, classroom patterned after British House of Commons.

George R. Thorne Hall, an auditorium, and Mrs. Rachel Mayer gave $800,000 to erect and endow the Levy Mayer Hall of Law. In 1925 the W. A. Wieboldt Foundation contributed half a million dollars for the construction of Wieboldt Hall for the use of the School of Commerce. At the same time Judge Elbert H. Gary, an alumnus and generous patron of the University, gave $360,000 to construct the Gary Law Library.

These developments greatly altered the character of the University. On May 8, 1925, in an atmosphere of enthusiastic optimism, ground-breaking ceremonies for the new buildings were held with the principal donors participating. President Scott correctly described the occasion as the most important in the University's history since the founding. Within two years the water front at Chicago Avenue on the Near North Side (in the old Streeterville district), was dominated by these new towers, most important of which was the Montgomery Ward Building, then the tallest university building in the nation. The "skyscraper campus" rapidly developed a character and social life of its own despite the fact that a large number of the students were taking evening courses. Student groups soon established a dozen fraternity chapters, and separate social and academic clubs.

Despite the success of the building campaign, some objectives had to be laid aside or postponed. Thorne Auditorium was not completed for several years and the construction of buildings for the schools of Music and Speech, as well as a new dormitory for the

CHICAGO WATER TOWER and Armory stood in background as excavation began on Ward building.

1926—SKELETON of Ward building took form rapidly. It became first skyscraper university structure in U.S.

MONTGOMERY WARD MEMORIAL building housed Schools of Medicine and Dentistry. Wesley Hospital at right.

women, had to be delayed for lack of funds. Nevertheless, one-half of the goal of $25,000,000 for the decade of the 1920's had been secured and the University had every reason to feel proud of its effort. It was estimated that nearly twenty million dollars would be needed in addition for a new library, a chapel, a new women's dormitory, a new men's dormitory, a women's building, science laboratories, buildings for the schools of Music, Speech, Journalism, and Education, and a stadium. A trustees' Committee on Development, with Melvin Traylor as chairman, and Thomas Gonser as executive secretary, after careful study decided that in the next financial campaign priority should be given to the needs of the cramped Evanston campus.

Through the initiative of Mark W. Cresap, alumnus and trustee of the University, and several other alumni, a new organization, called the Northwestern University Foundation, was formed in 1926 for the purpose of seeking financial support from alumni on an annual basis. This organization, now called the Alumni Fund, has become an increasingly important source of financial support for the University and has strengthened the bond between Northwestern and its alumni. Since 1926 some 17,000 alumni have made gifts to the University through the Alumni Fund.

With the new facilities, new methods and personnel were also introduced. As part of his revolutionary administrative policy, President Scott organized a department of Uni-

1924—PURPLE CANDLES were lighted for past, present, and future in annual rite. Dean Kent, Dean Holgate, Dean Cumnock, Mrs. Marie Swanson, Pres. Scott, Mrs. Helen Latham, Dean Lutkin, Dean Dennis, Charles Ward.

versity Personnel under Director L. B. Hopkins and a University Placement Bureau. In addition, he initiated a series of educational surveys among the University's schools in the year 1923-24. These surveys were valuable in clarifying the objectives of the schools and in determining how those objectives could be accomplished. The Board of Supervision of Student Activities was expanded to include the dean of men, the dean of women, a rep-

resentative from each school and the director of personnel.

The Chicago professional schools, whose physical equipment had been greatly enlarged, also expanded their academic activities. The Medical School increased its student enrollment through the use of the additional facilities which came with the occupancy of the Ward Memorial Building. In addition, the School transferred certain non-clinical science

N.U. BAND marched through University gates in Alumni Day Parade, watched by relatives and friends.

JAMES ALTON JAMES, professor of history and Graduate dean, gave devoted service to N.U.

courses offered in the first two years of medicine to the curriculum of the College of Liberal Arts.

The *Illinois Law Review*, published by the Northwestern University Press with a board of editors from the Law School, was united with the *Illinois Law Quarterly*, published by the University of Illinois. The new *Review*

HORACE GOODRICH, donor of University's giant candle, with President Scott at Candle-lighting 1928.

DEBATE TEAM OF 1924 continued tradition of oratorical success. Groups won many titles.

was first published in the fall of 1924 under the editorship of faculty members and students selected from the law schools of the University of Illinois, the University of Chicago and Northwestern University. (In 1932 Northwestern re-acquired full control of the publication and it was placed under student editorship.) In the same year the Institute for Research in Land Economics and Public Utilities was added to the School of Commerce and Dr. Richard T. Ely, famous economist and founder of the Institute, became Research Professor of Economics in that School.

In his annual report to the president for 1925, Dean James of the Graduate School emphasized the necessity for an increase in the number of graduate courses offered in certain departments, proper housing for graduate students and a fund to enable faculty members to carry on advanced instruction and research. An appeal was submitted to the

board of trustees on behalf of the Graduate School by Dean Raymond A. Kent, Professor Frederick S. Deibler and Dean James, in which it was stated: "We believe that the most essential step to be taken in the development of Northwestern University is a united campaign for the support and development of graduate work and research. . . ." They recommended a million-dollar endowment to encourage research, either by lightening the teaching load of the current faculty or by bringing scholars for the Graduate School from other institutions.

The importance of the teaching profession, and the need for adequate training of teachers, was reflected in the creation of a School of Education in 1926. It was housed in the Old College building, henceforth known as the Education Building, and Dr. John E. Stout was appointed first dean of the School. Courses brought within its jurisdiction included those which had been provided by the College of

OLD COLLEGE has stood through near century of varied uses; has served School of Education since 1926.

FAMILIAR SIGHT for students hurrying from "Tech" to South Campus was walk by Garrett Biblical Institute.

TWENTIETH CENTURY GOTHIC Seabury-Western Theological Seminary faced modern Technological Institute.

Liberal Arts through the departments of education and religious education, and by the School of Music and the School of Speech. The program for the School was at first limited to the junior and senior years and graduate work. At the same time the School was granted the right to recommend candidates for the degree of Master of Science in Education, and a similar power was granted to the Medill School of Journalism and to the School of Speech to grant the degrees of Master of Science in Journalism and Master of Science in Speech, respectively. The theatre department was organized in the School of Speech in 1926 by Alexander Dean and in 1928 the University Theatre was established as a single organization, consolidating the earlier play-producing organizations.

The College of Engineering, in 1925, adopted the policy that a majority of its teachers should henceforth be members of the engineering faculty. In the same year a general plan for "independent study" was substituted for "honors courses," which had been introduced by some departments of the College. Following a successful experiment in the College of Liberal Arts the plan for faculty advisers for freshmen was established in 1926.

The Western Theological Seminary of the Protestant Episcopal Church was assigned a

MARSHAL JOSEPH JOFFRE, victor of Battle of the Marne, was awarded honorary LL.D. by University in 1923.

site adjoining the campus in 1923, but it was not until 1928 that the present buildings were erected across Sheridan Road from Garrett Biblical Institute and not until 1933 that the institution merged with Seabury Seminary under the title of Seabury-Western.

The Alumni Association was granted an advisory function in the granting of honorary degrees in 1926. There were many notable visitors to the Northwestern campus during the 1920's. Madame Marie Curie and Marshal Joseph Joffre were awarded honorary

1934—CHOIR DIRECTORS' CONFERENCE met for singing in Evanston's First Congregational Church.

CONSTRUCTION OF DORMITORIES and sorority houses of Women's Campus went on rapidly during 1920's.

1926—COEDS HAD LARK and also did some useful work during construction of South Quadrangle houses.

degrees by the University, and such distinguished alumni as Dr. Charles Mayo, cofounder of the Mayo Clinic, and Glenn Frank, editor of the *Century Magazine* and soon to become president of the University of Wisconsin, were similarly honored.

Long-range expansion of the Evanston campus continued. The Women's Campus site was dedicated in June, 1926 and within a year two dormitories and fourteen sorority houses in the new quadrangle were ready for occupancy. Two dormitories, Rogers House and Hobart House, were built by the University for unaffiliated women, but the building of the sorority houses involved a long struggle characterized by a variety of money-making expedients on the part of the various chapters. Alpha Phi conducted the 'Cricket on the Hearth' tea room in the Carlson Building in Evanston, while Delta Gamma organized the 'Anchor Inn' at the Community Golf Course and Kappa Kappa Gamma appealed to the popular trade with 'George's Hot Dog Wagon.' The University Circle, whose successful foundation owed much to the efforts of Mrs. Walter Dill Scott and Mrs. James A. James, was also active in promoting the development of the Women's Campus.

A gift by the Carnegie Foundation enabled the Music School to develop a department of church music. In 1929 Milton H. Wilson, long a generous donor of money and services to the University, bequeathed $8,000,000 to the College of Liberal Arts. Two committees were appointed from the board of trustees and the faculty to determine the principles upon which the income was to be applied. Their report, "The Aim and Purpose of the College of Liberal Arts," recommended that the enrollment of the College be limited and that facilities for this limited number be improved.

In November, 1926, Northwestern's athletic facilities were increased with the completion of Dyche Stadium. Named after William A. Dyche, the University's business manager for many years, the new stadium had a seating

HORACE GOODRICH and Cornelia Lunt represented continuity of old Northwestern families and benefactors.

WORRIED FACES reflected momentary concern for home team at Big Ten game in Northwestern's Dyche Stadium.

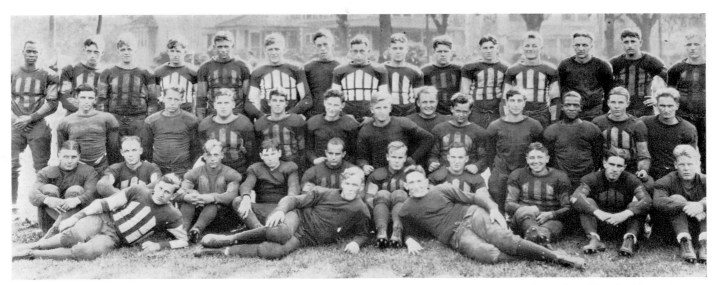

1926—FOOTBALL TEAM played usual rough schedule with vigor, won Big Ten championship for first time.

capacity of 47,000. To celebrate the opening, the football team defeated Chicago 37 to 7 and ended the season in a first-place Conference tie with Michigan. Throughout the 1920's, in fact, Northwestern football teams showed a steady improvement under the instruction of Glenn Thistlethwaite and in 1930 achieved the honor and the disappointment

PASSAVANT HOSPITAL, adjacent affiliated institution, was serviced largely by Medical School staff.

TRAFFIC INSTITUTE, University sponsored service school, annually trained policemen in latest methods.

of a defeat by Notre Dame for the national championship.

The Chicago Campus also benefited from the booming prosperity of the last half of the decade. In 1928 Passavant Hospital on the Chicago Campus opened with a staff composed from the faculty of the Medical School. Cooperation between the faculty and the hospital made possible the inauguration of a five-year combined course of study for nurses. At the same time the area of the Chicago Campus was increased to fourteen acres to provide space for future building.

In 1929 the Air Law Institute and the Scientific Crime Detection Laboratory were established in the Law School. At that time scientific detection was a new study in the United States and Northwestern's Crime Detection Laboratory achieved national fame with its application of science to Chicago's crime problem. Gradually the laboratory became less a research and more a service institution for police departments and other law

WARM DAYS OR COLD, Lt. McNamee gave lessons in marksmanship for members of women's rifle team.

enforcing agencies of Chicago and Illinois. Therefore negotiations were begun which resulted in the purchase of the laboratory by the City of Chicago in 1937.

A Naval Reserve Officers' Training Corps, one of six such units in the country, was established at the University in 1926, despite some anti-military sentiment in the city of Evanston. Naval officers taught courses in navigation, naval history, and other subjects designed to prepare students for commissions in the Naval Reserve. Commander Stephen B. McKinney was given charge of the new department of naval science and tactics and in 1927 a Navy Building was erected on the lake front north of Fisk Hall to provide classrooms and offices. The program for the Naval Unit became increasingly popular, and when the strength of the Army R.O.T.C. fell below the required government minimum of 100, the unit was abandoned in 1930.

The rapid, often turbulent progress of the age broke in on the academic calm of the

NROTC CADETS paraded proudly in review. Unit served as prototype in recent expansion of naval program.

COLORFUL MURALS, charcoal drawings, oil and water color paintings, and figure designs were included in exhibit.

University at ever-increasing intervals. The Age of Ballyhoo had its representatives on the campus, where trousers got longer, skirts shorter and hazing more violent. Indeed, one of the first and most serious problems with which Dr. Scott was called upon to deal was the famous Mount Case, in which a student mysteriously disappeared at the time of the traditional Freshman-Sophomore Rush in 1921. Subsequently all forms of hazing were prohibited by a pledge which every student must make upon matriculation.

Conventions and previous patterns of behavior were vigorously, although sometimes self-consciously, rejected. Charleston contests and raccoon coats became the rage, a few students pledged themselves not to bear arms in future wars and piles of cigarette butts out-

HEAVY JACKETS and raccoon coats failed to weigh down spirits of Northwesterners during winter in 1920's.

JOURNALISM students received expert instruction in reporting. They worked in realistic newspaper conditions.

126

1922—WOMEN'S Athletic Association presented annual musical reviews, predecessors of today's Waa-Mu shows.

"WHOA, THERE" said Joe Miller, director of 1930 show, as he gave instructions to three dancing coeds.

CHORUS GIRLS strutted as part of 1934 Waa-Mu show. By then review had become yearly extravaganza.

SHOW BUSINESS was satirized in 1949. Movies, radio and theatre were subjects of student-penned skits.

PLUMAGE and jewels failed to hide charms of coeds in "Hats Off," 1935 version presented at Loop theatre. 1948 show, "See How They Run," had political theme.

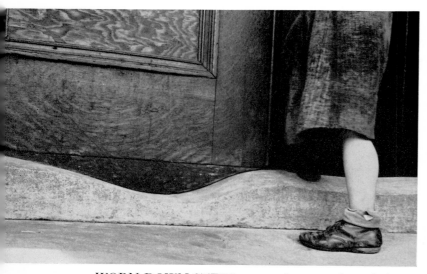

WORN DOWN STEPS, mute witness to feet of thousands who gained help from University Settlement House.

side the University gates bore witness to the University's tradition of no smoking on campus. Required chapel attendance was finally suspended, partly because of the lack of an adequate chapel. The *Syllabus* commented that in the *Purple Parrot* (founded in 1921), "All the naughty pictures have been kept out—most of them," and the *Syllabus* itself featured the somewhat controversial 'Cuts and Grinds' in its publication. The literary magazine, *Scrawl*, a sophisticated and artistic journal with a high cost and low circulation, was published during the last half of the decade but came to a sudden and unlamented end as a result of the depression.

As the sophistication of the Twenties reached its climax in 1929, Northwestern ventured into the world of musical comedy with the first WAA-MU show, 'Good Morning Glory' under the direction of Joe Miller, and its success "almost assured the campus of a mixed comedy as an annual event."

On February 9, 1929, a group of fifty-seven leading Chicagoans met to form a permanent organization called the Northwestern University Associates, with Silas H. Strawn, trustee and prominent Chicago attorney, as chairman. The group has been active and extraordinarily helpful in fostering the interests of the University among leading citizens of the community.

Many changes were made in the faculty—changes which increased with the organization of a system of sabbatical leaves and a

NORTHWESTERN MARCHING BAND performed in Chicago's Soldier Field during 1933 Century of Progress.

retirement plan. James E. Armstrong became dean of men and Irving S. Cutter the dean of the Medical School in 1925. John F. Hayford, director of the College of Engineering, died suddenly in 1925 and Kenneth Wilson became director of Athletics in the same year. The year 1928 saw more changes in the faculty. Dean Wigmore, Dean Lutkin and Professor Charles B. Atwell all retired and Dean Potter resigned. The religious activities of the Evanston students acquired a director in the person of James M. Yard, Augustus R. Hatton succeeded Norman Dwight Harris as chairman of the political science department and a young lecturer in contemporary Oriental civilization, William M. McGovern, startled students in Harris Hall with his unorthodox manner and headgear.

1928—WISTFUL COED QUEEN posed with oddly headgeared attendants during May Day celebrations.

The Great Depression, 1930-1939

The 1920's had been a decade of unusual change and growth, but it was almost forgotten as the cold autumn of 1929 deepened into the bleak economic winter of the 1930's. Efforts were primarily concentrated on a grim struggle for the maintenance of existing educational standards. Despite reassurances by the leaders of business and industry and despite such hopeful signs as the success of the Chicago Century of Progress in 1933, in which a number of Northwestern faculty members took an active part, there could be no doubt, as the depression steadily deepened month by month, that prosperity was not "right around the corner." Only courageous optimism could justify Dr. Scott's prediction in 1931 that "Within the next decade or two the Evanston campus will probably be extended eastward into the lake for a quarter or half a mile. East of the campus will probably be a lagoon and east of the lagoon a public park, a landing field and a boulevard."

Registration fell off sharply, scholarship and loan funds were drawn on heavily and deficits, which had disappeared for a time in the late 1920's, again appeared to plague the administration. Rigid economies became necessary

and faculty salaries suffered two cuts of ten per cent each between 1931 and 1933. New men of outstanding caliber could not be secured to fill vacancies. Seven departments in the faculty of the College of Liberal Arts were operated under temporary heads and the

1930—REGISTRATION for classes was much as it is today even though it took place in Old Patten Gym.

THORNE HALL, Chicago Campus auditorium, was completed in 1932. Mrs. George Thorne gave money for building.

POLE VAULT of 13 feet 9 11/16 inches won Big Ten Championship for Northwestern's Tom Warne in 1931.

normal course of appointments and promotions was postponed. Teaching schedules became heavier, purchase of essential equipment was delayed and appropriations for books and research were restricted. There was little satisfaction to be found in the thought that some other institutions in the country suffered even more severely. It was a time of disillusionment, in which nearly half the students worked their way, and in which the problems of the day seemed more important to students than social activities.

The completion of three buildings during the depression years was a major triumph for the University. George R. Thorne Hall, the much-needed auditorium for the Chicago Campus, was completed in 1932. The second building, the Charles Deering Library on the Evanston campus, was made possible by a bequest of the late Charles Deering and later

1932 — ROGER McCORMICK laid cornerstone for Deering Library. Mrs. Charles Deering stood third from left.

gifts by his wife, son, and two daughters, the whole amounting to approximately $1,000,000. During 1931 work was begun on the new building and the cornerstone was laid by Roger McCormick, grandson of Charles Deering, in January, 1932. Designed in Norman Gothic style, and including many unique features designed by Theodore W. Koch, the librarian, the beautiful new building provided space for a library which had become cramped in the Lunt Building. The latter structure was used for classrooms until 1935 when it was remodeled as an administrative building. It again reverted to a classroom building in 1941, when the administrative offices were transferred to their present building on Clark Street. An annex to Fisk Hall for the use of the zoology department, named in memory of Professor William A. Locy, was also completed in 1931.

During the depression no University department was abandoned and some were even expanded. A four-year curriculum for students in the School of Education was introduced in 1931. Prior to this time the first two years were completed by students of this School in the College of Liberal Arts. In order to make possible greater consideration

DEERING LIBRARY took place of Lunt whose space had become too cramped for University's many books.

of the interests and capacities of the individual student two types of bachelor's degrees were introduced in the College of Liberal Arts in 1932-33, an Honors Degree for students of

exceptional achievement and a Pass Degree for those with average records.

Increased demand for evening study in the fields of liberal arts, education and speech from

LUNT HALL SERVED as administrative headquarters during 1935-1941 period, then became classroom building.

UNTIL PATTEN was torn down to make room for Tech Building, commencement exercises were held there.

1925 on resulted in the establishment of University College on the Chicago Campus in 1933, with Samuel N. Stevens as director. The University thus reached a new and wider

1933—ESTABLISHMENT of University College provided evening study for people who worked during day.

clientele of business people, teachers and youth who could not attend college full time; enrollment grew rapidly. The School of Commerce did even more extensive evening work. The Summer School, operating on both campuses, expanded its offerings and served increasing numbers of public school teachers and regular students.

The Graduate School had over 1,000 students but still lacked adequate resources for research, a difficulty which could not be corrected during depression years. Despite this problem, the School was reorganized in preparation for a period of expansion. The Board of Graduate Studies was reconstituted in 1933 so as to make its membership more representative of the various schools. Later in the same year graduate work was more completely unified with the creation of a Graduate School Faculty in place of the Board of Graduate Studies. Appointments to the new faculty were limited to those who had given tangible

ILLUMINATION NIGHT furnished chance for students, alumni to get together each year in 1920's-30's.

TELETYPE MACHINE provided direct wire service from press associations for Medill journalism students.

evidence of their ability and interest in graduate work.

Various departments of the University scheduled a number of conferences on the Evanston campus during 1931. The social science departments arranged a two-day conference which was attended by members of university faculties from the entire Northwest. A conference of teachers of English from schools in the vicinity of Northwestern was held under the auspices of the English department and problems in the fields of elementary, secondary and junior college education were discussed in a series of conferences sponsored by the School of Education. The Northwestern University Social Science Research Council, organized in 1931, made major contributions to Northwestern's academic distinction through encouraging and systematizing research in its field.

The most widely debated event of the decade, however, and one which demonstrated more clearly than anything else the financial problems facing higher education in the diffi-

1938—KENNETH E. OLSON became dean of School of Journalism when it was separated from Commerce.

MERCHANDISING CLASS visited Chicago mail order house to study and take notes on methods and materials.

cult Thirties, was the proposal in 1933 to merge Northwestern and the University of Chicago. Initially, enthusiasm was expressed for the scheme. Dr. Scott declared that it was an opportunity to realize all three essentials of a well-rounded university: a great undergraduate college, a great graduate school and a group of great professional schools. President Robert M. Hutchins of the University of Chicago viewed the plan as a wise measure of economy and consolidation in a time of financial depression and an inspiring example of two private institutions amalgamating for the good of American education.

Committees were appointed to study the financial, legal and educational aspects of the merger. The reports of these committees were not nearly so optimistic as were the statements of the two presidents. No formal findings were presented but it was known that strong protests against the proposed merger had been expressed, in particular by the representatives of the medical and graduate schools. Finally, a majority of the board of trustees came out against it and the plan was laid aside.

The University carried out a number of other administrative and educational changes during the late 1930's. A central Office of Admissions was established for the Evanston schools and the College of Engineering curriculum was altered so as to permit greater specialization in engineering subjects. In order to provide a broad liberal arts background the School of Journalism moved to a five-year program in 1938 with a three-year pre-professional division. At the same time the School was separated from the School of Commerce with its own administration under Dean Kenneth E. Olson. In 1936 improvement in the administration of student affairs was effected with the reorganization of the Board of Student Activities.

Between January 1936 and June 1937 an all-University survey was conducted. Heretofore surveys had pertained to individual

SHAKESPEAREAN love sonnets were not out of place in Shakespeare Gardens near Garrett Biblical Institute.

schools but this survey covered all Northwestern at once. Five main sources of information were used—the history of the University, the previous surveys of the various schools, findings of special committees, individual opinions of persons associated with Northwestern and opinions of experts from other institutions. The report of the survey recommended the restoration of salary cuts made during the depression years, redefined the purpose of the University and drew up a plan for the reorganization of the administrative staff.

As early as 1902 President E. J. James had recommended that the functions of the presidency be separated and the duties entrusted to several officials. In 1937, as a result of the survey report, this recommendation was finally carried out. Franklyn B. Snyder, dean of the Graduate School, was appointed Vice-President and Dean of Faculties and Harry L. Wells, who had succeeded William A. Dyche

as business manager in 1934, became Vice-President and Business Manager.

The new business manager immediately conducted a comprehensive survey of all organizations not directly educational in their purposes. As a result major reorganizations in the athletic department, business office, management of dormitories and commons, and the educational administrative offices were authorized by the trustees, resulting in financial savings to the University as well as in greater effectiveness of administration.

The second generation of notable scholars and leaders in the history of Northwestern's faculty began to retire during the 1930's. Thomas F. Holgate, James T. Hatfield, George Oliver Curme and Henry Crew retired in 1933, James A. James in 1935, and John A. Scott, chairman of the department of classics since 1904, in 1938. New faces appeared. Fred D. Fagg, Jr. became dean of the School of Commerce and Dr. Charles W.

FRED FAGG, JR., was dean of Commerce, later vice president, now president of U. of Southern California.

demned scoffers who had thrown pennies on the stage and deplored the fact that it was necessary to bring in outside talent. Interest was also directed in 1937 to the fate of two enthusiastic freshmen who had been arrested for posting Charity Ball stickers on police squad cars, as well as to a Halloween encounter between students of the north and south quadrangles, in which the police were forced to use tear gas to disperse the fun-makers. During the period the University granted honorary degrees to such renowned visitors as Gutzon Borglum, Thomas Mann, William Allen White and Edgar Bergen.

The renaissance of Northwestern athletics, which began with the surge to the University's first Big Ten football championship in 1926, continued as the Wildcats tied for the title in 1930 and 1931, under the leadership of Coach Dick Hanley. Lynn Waldorf began a 12-year tenure as coach in 1935 and the following year the Purple again finished in first place.

Basketball also enjoyed a period of prosperity under the coaching guidance of "Dutch" Lonborg who joined the athletic staff in 1927 and turned out the University's first Big Ten

Freeman, dean of the Dental School in succession to Dr. Arthur D. Black, son of Dr. Greene Vardiman Black.

Despite the depression, or perhaps because of it, student official and social life increased in variety and interest. The Student Council was replaced by a Student Governing Board under the authority of the Evanston Campus Association. Social affairs, such as the Junior Prom, the Military Ball and the Charity Ball featured the artistry of Jan Garber, Harry Sosnick and Clyde McCoy as well as the illustrious local talent of Joe Miller and his orchestra. The senior class of 1935 set a precedent by holding the Senior Ball in the Loop at the Palmer House. The *Daily Northwestern*, reduced to tabloid size as a result of the depression, began a Chicago Campus news section in 1935, with articles such as one on television ("Still in Experimental Stages, says N. U. Professor"). Commenting editorially on the 1937 WAA-MU Show, the *Daily* con-

EDGAR BERGEN, Northwestern alumnus and originator of Charlie McCarthy, awarded honorary degree.

137

1937—COEDS left sorority house for class.

TABLET by Avenue of Elms was dedicated to World War I heroes.

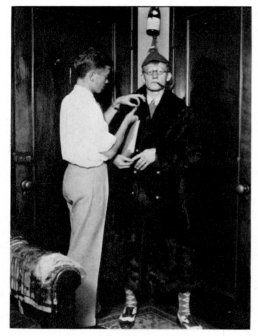

FROSH decided to pledge fraternity.

CIDER AND DOUGHNUTS provided informal spread at midnight.

VISITORS welcomed to Austin House.

"GONE WITH THE WIND" gained 1936 coeds' attention.

1931—GRID SQUAD tied for Big Ten Title. Dick Hanley coached Wildcats to other crowns in 1926, 1930.

TOM ROBINSON coached swim teams from 1910-1943, gained 10 Big Ten titles. This was his last team.

1930—STUDENTS gathered about bonfire and cheered football team which shared Big Ten championship.

championship basketball team in 1931. The Wildcats won the title again in 1933 as Captain Joe Reiff won the Conference individual scoring championship for the second time.

Meanwhile the swimming team maintained the long series of successes which had been inaugurated back in 1910 when Tom Robinson became coach. During a brilliant career, which ended with his retirement in 1943, Coach Robinson compiled an unsurpassed record of 10 Big Ten championships and five national titles.

All too slowly the tide of depression receded. In 1936 the University budget was balanced for the first time in six years and by 1937 the enrollment of students was again on the in-

MASKED COEDS received pointers from clowns while appearing in Circus.

PROCEEDS FROM 1933 CIRCUS "Purple Carnival," a regulation three-ring extravaganza, went to University's Student Loan Fund.

FERRIS WHEELS, carousels, exciting rides, and booths filled annual circus site near North Quads.

1932—SORORITY FLOAT with bass drum and soldiers commemorated 25th anniversary of N.U. circus.

"TRAINED WILD RABBITS" in form of Northwestern coeds, performed under canvas in 1932 version.

MUSCULAR and loyal slaves accompanied elaborately-bedecked soldier riding pony-drawn Roman chariot.

ROGER DEERING left Northwestern $7,000,000 in 1937 for general use and development of University.

EXUBERANT students celebrated Wildcats' 14-7 football victory in 1935 over Notre Dame, a rare occasion.

crease. In 1937 Northwestern also received the bequest of Roger Deering of $7,000,000 to be devoted to general development. Since the first gift by William Deering in 1876, seven members of the family, including his sons Charles and James, had made seventy different gifts or bequests to the University, amounting to a total of more than $10,500,000.

The Department of Development, founded in 1933 to plan for the future, was prepared to take advantage of the better times. The Century Plan, first announced late in 1936, was a challenge to all the friends of Northwestern. It was a program of building and academic improvement for the next fifteen years, which was to reach its climax in 1951 with the proposed Centennial celebration. The Plan was largely the work of Fred W. Sargent, chairman of the trustees' Committee on Development and Thomas A. Gonser, director of the Department of Development. Primary objectives included the construction of adequate dormitories on both campuses, increased support for research, and a number

SWIMMING TEAM, which won five national crowns, played host to other schools in Patten Gymnasium pool.

1936—FOOTBALL team won title. Backfield stars Jefferson, Vanzo, Geyer, Heap, and Adelman led attack.

1936—REPUBLICAN boosters campaigned for candidate in Mock Political Convention, quadrennial school event.

FRED W. SARGENT was University trustee. He began Century Plan in 1936.

THOMAS A. GONSER was vice-president and public relations director.

of important buildings, among them a general hospital and a children's hospital on the Chicago Campus, and in Evanston a student union building, an engineering quadrangle, a chapel and buildings for the schools of Education, Commerce, Music and Journalism. It was hoped that the total assets of Northwestern would reach the $100,000,000 mark by the University's hundredth year.

During the first year of the Century Plan the University secured gifts of nearly two and a half million dollars. Particularly important were gifts from the estate of LaVerne Noyes, and from the widow and sons of the late Milton J. Florsheim, a University trustee. The University was better prepared to take

1932—NORTHWESTERN and President Scott welcomed "precocious students," 14-15 year-old freshmen.

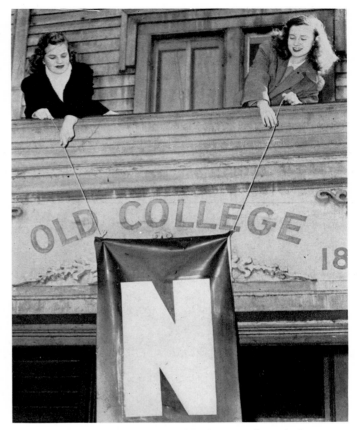

SMILING COEDS HUNG "N" banner from balcony of Old College, only building ever to win "N" award.

"GIRL OF THE GOLDEN WEST," Belasco melodrama, was 1935 production of Univ. Theater Players.

advantage of its improved fortunes than it had been before the depression, for necessity had forced increased efficiency in business administration. By 1938 the budget showed a small surplus which was laid aside as an equalization reserve.

In June, 1938, official announcement of the Centennial celebration for 1951 was made. Among the features of the program recommended were a history of Northwestern's first hundred years, a plan for the contribution to be made by the University toward the future development of higher education in the United States and a conference of leading scholars for the promotion of learning in various fields.

The recovery from the depression was almost complete and in 1938 the University initiated a building program which would double existing classroom space on the Evanston campus and more than double the total open dormitory accommodations. Five fraternity houses were completed on the north campus. The Chicago Campus moved a step nearer completion with the erection of the "skyscraper dormitory," Abbott Hall. It was donated by Dr. Wallace C. Abbott, a prom-

1938—ABBOTT HALL, Chicago Campus dorm., was memorial to Dr. Wallace Abbott, prominent physician.

inent physician of Chicago, and his wife Clara A. Abbott, through the Clara A. Abbott Trust. The income from this eighteen-story dormitory, social and recreational center for some eight hundred students of the professional schools, was to be devoted to the promotion of research in the medical, surgical and chemical sciences. In the same year old Willard Hall, which was no longer suitable for living quarters, was replaced by a new Willard Hall at the west end of the Women's Campus.

In March, 1939, President Scott announced to the Board of Trustees that he was asking their acceptance of "the largest gift [not bequest] ever received by Northwestern University at any one time." The gift was one of $6,735,000 by the Walter P. Murphy Foundation and it was to be used to establish the Northwestern Technological Institute. The announcement came as a climax to three

MODERNITY was theme of architects who designed Abbott Hall. Lounge, student rooms were comfortable.

SPACIOUS DINING ROOM and cafeteria offered excellent eating facilities to Chicago Campus students.

with whom the problems of establishing an engineering school might be discussed. Charles F. Kettering, vice-president of General Motors Corporation and an advocate of the cooperative form of education which Mr. Murphy favored, became one of the investigators. Dean Herman P. Schneider of the School of Engineering of the University of Cincinnati, the originator of the cooperative plan in engineering

WALTER MURPHY, railroad supply manufacturer, donated over $30,000,000 to establishment of Tech Inst.

years of negotiation, during which the suitability of Northwestern as a site for the proposed institution was compared with that of a number of other universities.

Mr. Murphy's representative, Royall E. Cabell, had requested that the names of a few prominent engineers should be suggested,

PRESIDENT SNYDER, Charles F. Kettering, V. K. Zworykin, and William Knudsen inspect testing machine.

1939—PRESIDENT SCOTT held spade in groundbreaking ceremonies for Chicago Campus dormitory.

1938—NEW WILLARD HALL at west end of South Quadrangles became living quarters for freshman women.

PLANNING BOARD for Technological Institute included (top) Ralph Budd, Ovid Eshbach, Charles F. Kettering, Walter Dill Scott, Raymond C. Wieboldt, Paul E. Klopsteg, and (bottom) Robert E. Doherty, Robert E. Wood, William E. Wickenden, Henry J. Kaiser, James M. Barker, Robert A. Millikan, and Franklyn Bliss Snyder.

TECH STUDENTS "on Coop" worked at Chicago industrial firm. Dean Eshbach was in charge of program.

education, was employed as a consultant. Both favored creating the Institute in the Middle West and Northwestern, because of its sound business management and its proximity to Chicago, was found particularly suitable. In August, 1938, Mr. Cabell had informed the trustees of Northwestern that his "principal" was prepared to proceed with the plan to build a new school of engineering at Northwestern provided the cooperative system was adopted. Under this system students would alternate a quarter spent on actual engineering projects as employees of private companies with a quarter of training in the Institute. A contract was signed seven months later for the erection of the first unit of the Technological Institute which was to be supported by the Murphy Foundation for a five-year experimental period. Ovid Wallace Eshbach, able educator, engineer and authority on industrial personnel, was elected first dean of the new school.

President Walter Dill Scott described the project as "one of the most significant opportunities open to higher education in the last forty years, and we are deeply sensible of both the honor and the obligation which at-

PATTEN GYM was razed and Dearborn Observatory moved to make room for construction of Tech Institute in 1940.

taches to this gift . . ." A number of problems in connection with the design of the Institute were gradually solved and early in 1940 construction was begun. Unfortunately it was found necessary to raze the Patten Gymnasium to make room for the new building. Dearborn Observatory, also on the proposed site, was moved to the lake shore, at the mouth of the old Rubicon stream. A new gymnasium, named in honor of James A. Patten, the benefactor of the old gymnasium, was built north of the men's quadrangles.

In January, 1939, it was announced that Dr. Scott would retire in the following September, after nineteen years as president of the University. Not since its foundation had the University been administered by a president so completely identified with Northwestern and its development as Walter Dill Scott. The story of his great achievement is reflected in statistics of the University's growth. Between 1920 and 1939 the student

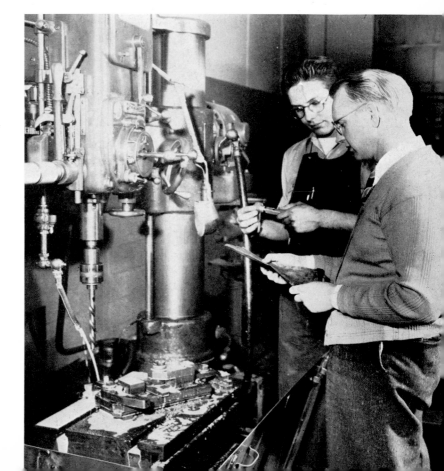

1851 AND ON—local "Rubicon" helped drain north-eastern Evanston, last vestige eliminated for Tech.

1940—PATTEN GYMNASIUM was more impressive sacrifice when its site was required for new structure.

DEARBORN OBSERVATORY, though sturdy stone, was spared by moving operation to new location near lake.

1940—EXCAVATION went rapidly after removal of older buildings. Bahai Temple, lighthouse on skyline.

PLANKS, GIRDERS, bricks and cranes, filled excavation as construction workers pushed erection of Tech Inst.

EFFECTIVE PATTERNS of steel were created as structure began to take form.

HOPES for swift completion were shattered when fire struck unfinished building.

1941—TECHNOLOGICAL INSTITUTE moved into nearly completed building of massive, modern design.

WARM WELCOME always awaited alumni who dropped in to visit President Scott at homecoming time.

"NORTHWESTERN for Her pretty girls," time-proven slogan, exemplified by 1938 May Queen and Court.

enrollment, including full and part-time and the summer session, had increased from 7,840 to 21,924 and the teaching staff from 490 to 1,254. The number of degrees granted increased fivefold and the University's resources rose from twelve million to almost fifty-four million dollars. The influence of the president and his wife on the more unobtrusive aspects of the University was likewise profound.

The Board of Trustees' Appreciation of Dr. Scott declared: "Northwestern University during his administration has moved forward from a relatively small institution which lacked general recognition for the good work it was doing to a place of magnificent buildings, enlarged endowment, and increased scholastic standards and has become a visual expression of a great university to the entire region in which it is located and the nation at large. . . . During this period Dr. Scott has established the intellectual integrity of the University in the public mind, and has been a

SELLING SANDWICHES for Scott Hall Fund was popular money raising method for quarter century.

NORTH SHORE MUSIC FESTIVAL once met under canvas in Dyche Stadium, but rain was not restrained.

wise and consistent defender of the principle of academic freedom."

A committee of Chicago and North Shore citizens under the leadership of trustee Harold H. Anderson, former president of the Northwestern University Alumni Association, laid plans to erect a memorial to Dr. and Mrs. Scott. This memorial took the form of a

student union building, for which $750,000 was solicited. The campaign, which owed much to the guidance of Vice-President Harry Wells, was a remarkable and immediate success. A Women's Building Association, organized in 1915 under the leadership of Mrs. James A. James and Mrs. Arthur Swanson, had been raising funds for a women's building.

SCOTT HALL with recreational, dining, and study facilities, completed east quadrangle in traditional Lannon stone.

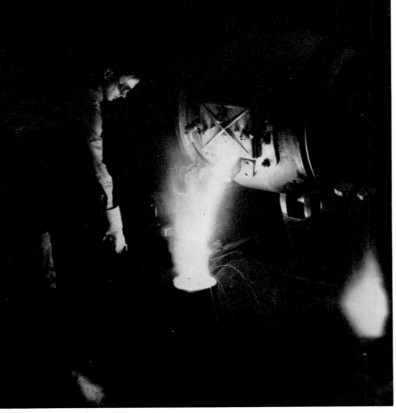

MOLTEN CAST IRON was drawn from electric furnace in Mechanical Engineering lab for testing analysis.

GLASS BLOWING, no job for amateurs, created specialized laboratory equipment for scientific research.

DR. V. N. IPATIEFF watched progress of experiment in high pressure laboratory bearing his name.

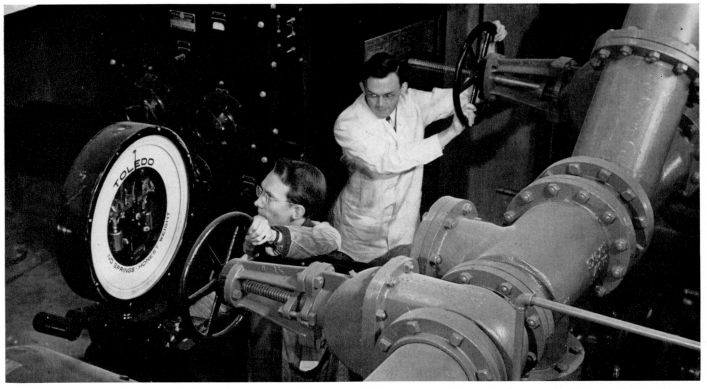

FLUID MECHANICS, studied in hydraulics laboratory. Water pumped from tank to tank illustrated principles.

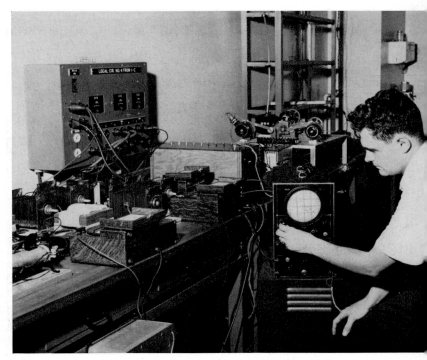

CATHODE RAY OSCILLOGRAPH, basis for television receiver, was checked by electrical engineer grad.

FOUR CHEMICAL ENGINEERS controlled and recorded data on evaporation process in unit operations lab.

OLIVER LEE, professor of astronomy, bargained over purchase of sandwich for lunch and union building.

The account of their efforts to raise funds, with its story of selling hot dogs at football games, operating a tea room in University Hall, laundering curtains, giving plays and undertaking a half hundred other expedients, is an inspiring one. On the announcement of the campaign for the Scott Memorial the Association offered to contribute its hard-earned fund of $165,106. A part of this fund had been raised earlier by women students and faculty wives by selling pencil sharpeners, hair shampoos, phonograph records, and countless sandwiches between classes on campus (which caused the press to refer to Scott Hall as the first building in the world "to be erected on a foundation of sandwiches.") Bertram Cahn, a University trustee, generously contributed $100,000 for the auditorium in Scott Hall. Several hundred dollars were raised through plays and operas presented by the University Circle and the WAA-MU donated the profits on its 1939 presentation. Finally it was announced, at the end of April, 1939, that $700,000 had been pledged and that the goal of breaking ground on Dr. Scott's seventieth birthday, May 1, would be achieved.

War Years, 1939-1945

On Dr. Scott's retirement in September, 1939, Franklyn B. Snyder, dean and vice-president, became the University's eleventh president with Fred Dow Fagg Jr. as Vice-President and Dean of Faculties. The installation ceremonies were held on September 1, 1939. War, which had hung over the 1930's like a black cloud and which was to dominate over half the years of Dr. Snyder's administration, had already broken out. For the moment, however, there was an uneasy Indian summer of peace in America and the University set itself to carry out President Snyder's plan of doing "everything in our power to bring all our schools and departments up to the high level of educational distinction already attained by the best."

The first freshman class for the Technological Institute was enrolled in 1939 as the massive structure continued to rise from its broad foundations on the north campus.

1941—WESLEY HOSPITAL was completed opposite Medical School. Unique design gave maximum sunlight.

Building progress was only slightly delayed by a fire in 1940 which caused $600,000 worth of damage to the uncompleted structure.

The University published a brochure, "Rounding Out a Century," in which the basic opportunities open to Northwestern were presented as a challenge at the end of its first century. Scott Hall, Abbott Hall and the new Patten Gymnasium were completed and the cornerstone was laid for the Wesley Memorial Hospital on the Chicago Campus. The Music School, under its new dean, John W. Beattie, was expanded with the acquisition of old Willard Hall and the erection in 1941 of Lutkin Hall, a recital auditorium.

Large donations were received for medical education and research. A $400,000 bequest to the University by the late Dr. John S. Appleman, a member of the Northwestern Associates, brought his total benefactions to the University to $635,000, of which $135,000 was restricted to the use of the Medical School clinics. At the same time Colonel Robert R. McCormick endowed the Irving S. Cutter Fund for medical research and the

TALENTS OF Music School faculty and students were displayed in Lutkin Hall, named after first dean.

EX-PRESIDENT Herbert Hoover attended 1940 Northwestern-Indiana game in Dyche Stadium. N.U. won 20-7.

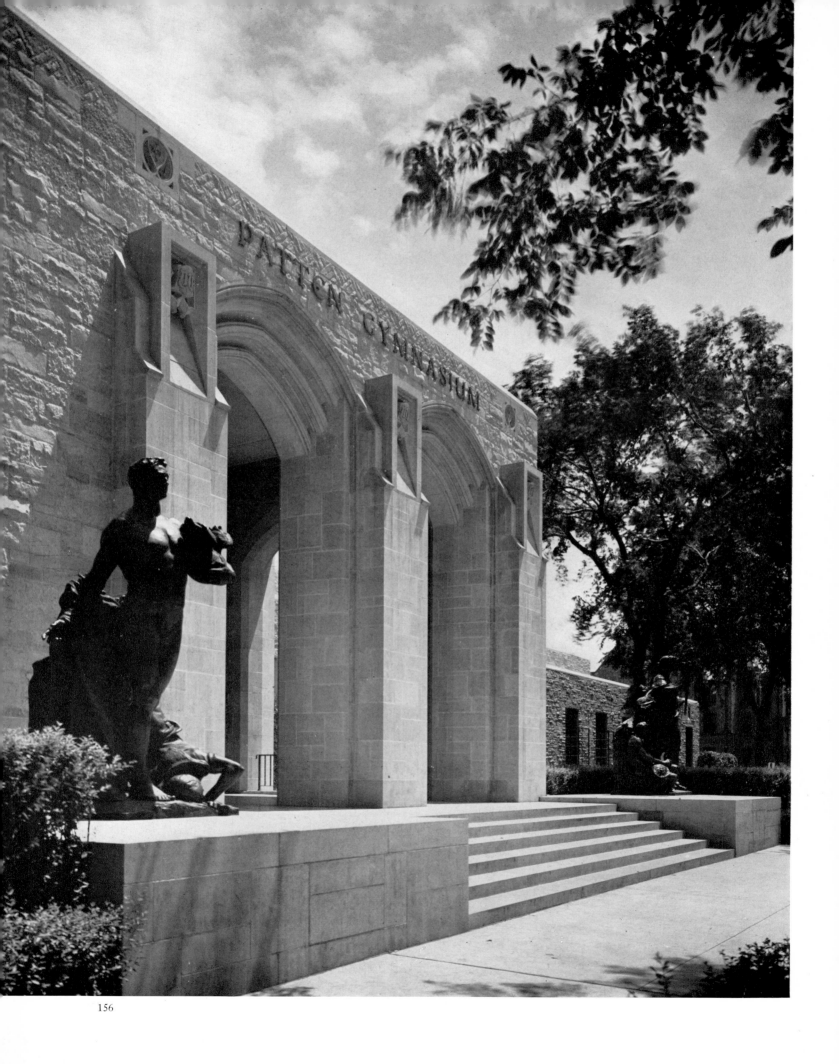

1940—JUBILATION marked students' faces as they snake-danced after second win since 1901 over Notre Dame.

Harry L. Wells
Business Manager—1937
Vice-President 1937—

Clara A. Abbott Trust added $162,000 to its original gift "to benefit the cause of medical, surgical and chemical science." In the following year Mrs. Joy Morton willed $2,000,000 to be used to construct another hospital on the Chicago Campus.

The principal interest of the times, however, was the war. André Geraud ("Pertinax"), the famous French journalist, delivered the Harris lectures on the Fall of France in December, 1940, and in the spring of 1941 a Northwestern Peace Week was organized to discuss the possibility of keeping the country out of war. In the summer of 1940 President Snyder had forehandedly appointed a committee to study all the facilities of the University which could be placed at the disposal of the government in time of war. The Civil Aeronautics Authority flying course which, under the sponsorship of the School of Commerce, had become the third largest in the country between 1939 and 1941, was transferred to the War Department. The Navy Department organized its Reserve Midshipmen's Training Unit in Abbott and Wieboldt Halls, and the Medical School, at the request of the Surgeon General of the United States Army, completed plans for organizing and staffing at short notice a complete army base hospital unit. In the autumn of 1940 the first selective service registration was undertaken, with the assistance of members of the staff. Fifteen hundred students on both campuses were registered.

In the middle of the academic year 1941-

158

1941—DECEMBER 7—PEARL HARBOR exploded ships, blew U.S. into war, changed character of University life.

42 came the news of Pearl Harbor and the American entry into World War II. All through that terrible winter, as the air waves filled with the news of the fall of Pacific islands, the angry nation and its universities mobilized. Northwestern University, remembering the mistakes of 1917, was faced with the problem, "How can the University contribute in every possible way to winning the war, and at the same time preserve the fundamentals of its many-sided educational program unimpaired, and also get itself in readiness to take full advantage of the opportunities and obligations which the return of peace will present?"

MEDICAL SCHOOL students practiced operation procedures with up-to-date equipment at Wesley Hospital.

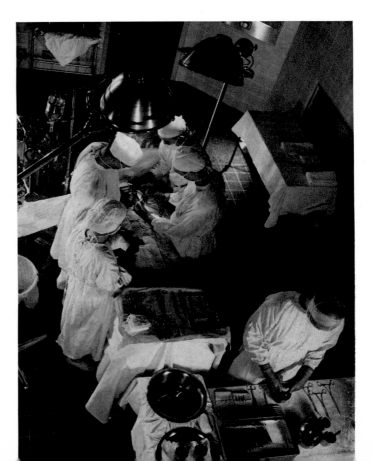

NAVY TOOK OVER large part of University. Midshipmen studied latest techniques in radio training program.

1943—U. S. NAVAL RESERVE MEN from Abbott Hall received diplomas in commencement exercises.

Early in 1942 the Medical School's new General Hospital No. 12 was ready for duty, while the Medical School devoted much of its research to national defense projects, notably in the case of the penicillin laboratory, founded in 1943 under the direction of Dr. C. J. Farmer. The campus rapidly became one of the chief centers of naval activity in the country. As in 1918, buildings on the Evanston campus were turned over to the forces, with Lunt and Swift Hall serving as barracks for a naval radio school and Foster House as a sick bay and dispensary. Other dormitories and fraternity houses were loaned to the Naval College Training Program, referred to as V-12.

In addition to making such special contributions, Northwestern cooperated with the

1942—NAVAL RADIO OPERATORS gathered in Cahn Auditorium to receive instruction from training leaders.

1944—NAVY V-12 MEN, 1,050 in number, paraded on Deering Meadow for visiting Navy and Marine Corps officers.

scientific branches of the armed forces in filling government contracts for defense research and many of the University laboratories were classified as restricted areas.

BLOOD BANK DONORS gave quantities of blood through unit established in lounge of Scott Hall.

"CIVILIAN DEFENSE" was work of Northwestern coeds who attended U.S.O. dances at Fort Sheridan.

HIGH SCHOOL INSTITUTES brought young students to summer sessions of Speech and Journalism.

On November 22, 1943, one of the important Army Civil Affairs Training Schools was in-augurated at Northwestern. Instruction was concentrated on language, area characteristics and civil affairs problems of first Germany and then Japan. Rollin B. Posey, director of University College, was made director of the school and Colonel Brown Rolston was liaison officer. Professor Curt R. Goedsche made a noteworthy success in the application of modern language study techniques, and several other faculty members taught for the "CATS."

Nearly 50,000 men and women came in contact with Northwestern as a training center and many war leaders, among them Admirals Ernest J. King and Chester W. Nimitz and General Omar Bradley, visited the campus. Four hundred faculty members left the campus for war service and more than fifteen thousand alumni and former students

GERMANY AND JAPAN were subjects for intensive study and training in four special C.A.T. Schools at N.U.

D-DAY—American soldiers hit Normandy shore under heavy fire. Numerous N.U. students saw action in landing.

served with the armed forces. Three hundred Northwesterners of all ranks died in the service and the following citations for the Congressional Medal of Honor are among the proud lines in Northwestern's history:

John L. Jerstad (School of Education, 1940); Major U.S.A.A.F. Killed in action, August 1, 1943, while leading, as a volunteer, a bombing mission over the Ploesti oil fields.

Walter E. Truemper (School of Commerce, 1941); Second Lieutenant, U.S.A.A.F. Killed, February 20, 1944, while returning from a bombing mission over Germany.

The restrictions of war had an immediate impact upon the student body. Cokes were rationed in the grill of Scott Hall, a short-lived "Kissing Must Stop" campaign was sacrificed to the war effort and off-campus social functions were cancelled for the duration. In view of the limitations placed on transportation by gas rationing, a Scott Hall Night Club was organized in the Grill by the Scott Hall Committee. Men rapidly disappeared from the campus and most of those who appeared at campus dances were in uniform. Fraternities barely maintained their identity; young women edited the *Daily Northwestern*, and carried on some other campus activities.

The Student Governing Board changed the name of its Student Defense Commission to the War Council and the latter conducted a number of war bond drives. More than thirty thousand dollars was subscribed to the first of these and Northwestern students gave 152 pints of blood in one day when the Blood

STUDENT DRAFTEES, bags in hand, said goodbye to Northwestern and campus on way to training camps.

1946—ADMIRAL CHESTER W. NIMITZ received honorary Doctor of Laws degree from President Snyder.

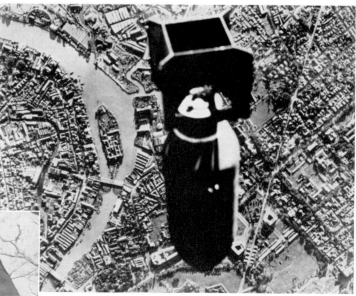

1942—CANNON, which honored N.U. men who fought in Civil War, was donated as scrap iron to use in making bombs for World War II.

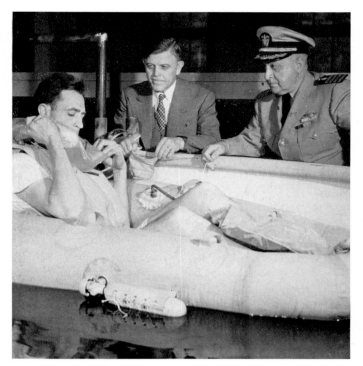

1943—PHARMACIST'S MATE tested life raft equipment as Dr. Andrew Ivy and Capt. W. L. Mann watched.

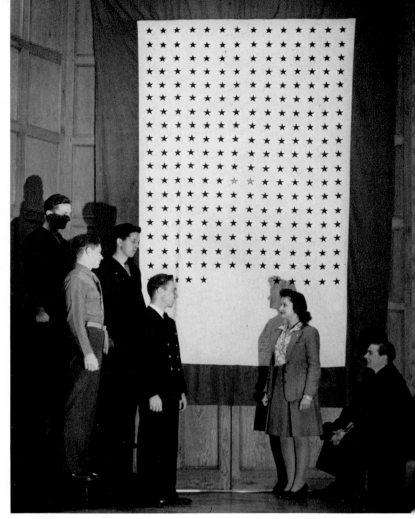

SCHOOL OF MUSIC unveiled its own service flag in ceremony of 1943; showed fraction of ultimate total.

VETERANS OF South Pacific fighting enrolled in V-12 officer training program.

SIGHTING BIG DECK GUN was important part of training in Abbott Hall gymnasium.

1945—NAVY WAS STILL in evidence when 87th graduation ceremonies were held on Deering Meadow.

V-12 MEN fought for ball in water targetball, game invented by Swim Coach Bill Peterson who looked on.

Donors Unit visited the campus. The Dolphin Club transferred funds raised through its shows from support of the swimming team to the war bond drive and the WAA-MU show disappeared for the duration. The war effort was also not without its humorous aspects. The Sixth War Loan was aided by a War Bond Carnival where sorority girls sold war stamps for admission to booths and professors acted as taxi dancers. President Snyder patriotically promised to carry the books for one day of the coed who bid highest, in terms of war bonds, for his services.

As in the period 1917-1918, the departure of a number of the faculty for war service placed added strain upon those who remained. Professors assumed additional teaching loads and improvisation was necessary to maintain Northwestern's educational standards. Not only was Northwestern able to hold its own in most spheres of activity but a number of innovations were made. An eleven-week summer session was scheduled to speed up the education of those students under military training.

During the war years the curriculum of the various schools remained more or less unchanged but toward the end of the war, and increasingly after 1945, new directions were plotted. In addition to strengthening many of its departments through new appointments, the College of Liberal Arts instituted in 1944 a new program for the Bachelor of Arts degree, widely hailed at the time as a great advance toward the ideal of a liberal education. This was a carefully planned sequence of sixteen units to be completed in four years of resident study, organized by a board composed of Professors G. Donald Hudson, Melville Herskovits and Bergen Evans. Half of these units were the same for all students and half were adaptable to the individual's special interests. As Bergen Evans stated, the

MAGNETIC BALANCE APPARATUS, developed by Professor Pierce Selwood for research with non-metals.

1945—SEPTEMBER 2—Shigemitsu signed Japanese surrender on U.S.S. *Missouri*. Veterans streamed back to school

MANY NORTHWESTERN STUDENTS lost lives in Allied victory in World War II.

drawing to a close and plans were made to convert the University to a peacetime establishment as rapidly as possible after the cessation of hostilities. On August 14, 1945, the World War came to an end and these plans were at once put into operation. It was expected in all the universities of the nation that enrollments would mount as a result of the G. I. Bill of Rights, but the magnitude of the increase had not been foreseen. The University was soon in danger of being swamped by student veterans. Additional problems were presented to the administration by the need to repair and replace facilities which had been destroyed or had worn out as a result of constant wartime use. Living accommodation used by the forces also had to be renovated before being returned to civilian use.

The war years had seen widespread changes in the faculty. Isaac Joslin Cox, well-known historian of Latin America, retired in 1941. In 1943 Paul Haensel, professor of economics and former economic adviser to the Russian government, and Arthur S. Todd, chairman of the department of sociology, also retired. The office of dean of students came into existence in 1943 with F. George Seulberger as first dean. Jens Nyholm was appointed University Librarian in April, 1944, succeeding Theodore Koch who had died in 1941. The close of the war brought even greater

changes. Addison Hibbard, dean of the College of Liberal Arts and Thomas F. Holgate, former president ad interim of the University, died in 1945. In the same year Ward V. Evans, chairman of the department of chemistry and expert on high explosives, retired, and Ted Payseur succeeded Kenneth Wilson as director of athletics. Simeon Leland, formerly chairman of the department of economics at the University of Chicago, was appointed professor of economics and dean of the College of Liberal Arts in 1946.

Fulfillment and Preparation, 1945-1951

The new academic year opened with nearly a thousand student veterans enrolled and these had increased by the spring quarter of 1946 to more than 6,000. During the year 1946-47, 12,033 veterans were enrolled on the two campuses and the total University enrollment reached a record of more than 29,000 full-time and part-time students. The admission of this increased number was not profitable economics for the University, but it was difficult to restrict registration in view of Northwestern's obligation to do all that it fairly could for the returned veterans. A system

NORTHWESTERN LEADERS sat with Trustee Burgess at football game—Presidents Snyder, Scott, and Miller.

of priorities was instituted to deal with the monumental problem of applications for admission, and about 2,000 freshmen were selected on the basis of merit from among five times that many applicants.

Increased accommodation was provided by 146 Quonset and Steel-craft huts and by the building of the $3,000,000 Northwestern Apartments, the largest housing unit in Evanston.

An addition to Swift Hall was constructed in 1945 to house the naval training program. The new building's equipment included a 5-inch naval gun and an 11-ton direction finder.

An even more important concern of the administration was to strengthen the faculties of the various schools to meet post-war demands. The primary requirement was that

ROBERT McCORMICK, alumnus, editor of *Chicago Tribune*, spoke in Cahn to Ney MacMinn's English class.

171

1946—HUTS were constructed to house increased post-war enrollments.

VETERAN AND FAMILY moved into one of 146 new steel huts on campus.

FAMILIES MADE tin can-like dwellings into comfortable living places.

APARTMENTS, Evanston's largest housing unit, was built to provide living accommodations for faculty families.

NAVAL OFFICERS presented clock award to President Franklyn B. Snyder in behalf of NROTC unit.

the new faculty personnel must be of the highest quality available. On the basis of this criterion expansion of numbers was large but undertaken with caution, keeping in mind the inevitable falling-off in student enrollment

once the post-war rush was over. Much of the increase would have taken place in the normal course of events. The years just before the war showed rising percentages of high school graduates going on to college and indicated a trend which the sudden return of the veterans in 1946 merely accentuated. More and more college graduates were also continuing into advanced study. By 1948-49 the peak of the veteran enrollment was apparently passing but the civilian load was increasing appreciably. In the words of President Snyder: "It seems indisputable that higher education must accustom itself to dealing with many more students than were in college before the war."

With the coming of peace, campus life settled down again into a refreshing, if markedly altered, state of normality.

Athletics, and particularly football, underwent a revival as many ex-servicemen returned to fill rosters depleted during the war. After the 1946 football season Lynn Waldorf resigned as football coach to become coach

1948—JOY AND VACATION were given students for gridders' selection to represent Big Nine in Rose Bowl.

TEAM, LED by All-American Art Murakowski, full-back, and Captain Alex Sarkesian, center, practiced.

STUDENTS accompanied team to California, had jam session in baggage car of Centennial Wildcat Special.

VICKY ERICKSON, N.U. coed, represented school on Big Nine float in colorful Rose Bowl Pageant parade.

WILDCATS SHOWED rival, University of California, that Midwest Conference was tough. N.U. won 20-14.

WRESTLING TOOK its place on athletic calendar. Coach Jack Riley watched team in rugged practice. ➤

at the University of California. He was replaced by a former pupil, Bob Voigts, who had won All-American honors in 1938. In his second year as coach, Voigts led the Wildcats to the Rose Bowl where they defeated the Waldorf-coached California Golden Bears, 20 to 14.

Two members of Northwestern's athletic teams, Bill Porter, track, and Bill Heusner, swimming, were members of the United States Olympic team that competed in London in 1948. Porter climaxed a brilliant career by winning the 110 meter hurdles Olympic championship in the record time of 13.9 seconds. Starting in 1947, the tennis team won four straight Big Ten championships. Ted Petersen won the conference singles title in 1947 and 1949 and Grant Golden was the winner in 1950. Other Northwestern teams which won Conference championships during the postwar period were golf, 1948, and fencing, 1947 and 1948.

The sobering influences provided by the war and the more mature outlook of the older student veterans began to disappear as the veteran enrollment declined. Freshmen were, for the most part, directly from high school and a more normal ratio of men to women was being re-established. WAA-MU

ARTHUR "DUTCH" LONBORG coached N.U. basketball teams for many years. Squads won many games.

GOLF COURSE belonging to University offered golf teams excellent facilities. Team won title in 1948.

HAROLD STASSEN spoke at 1948 mock convention. Senators Douglas, Illinois, and Morse, Oregon, did too.

UNIVERSITY THEATRE actors dressed and made up for presentation of Shakespearian costume play.

RADIO STUDENTS broadcast on station WNUR while faculty members Butler and Feddersen looked on.

COED PRACTICE TEACHER taught and played with three youngsters at North shore elementary school.

was revived with the show "Here We Go Again" and the Senior class held a costume ball with Duke Ellington providing the music.

THREE PRESIDENT'S WIVES chat at Pres. Miller's inauguration—Mrs. Scott, Mrs. Snyder, Mrs. Miller.

Publications temporarily increased in number with the printing of the short-lived *Pegasus*, which was merged with *Purple Parrot* in 1948. Freshman "beanies," voted down by the veterans, returned to the campus.

In August, 1949, in conformity with the University's retirement policy, Dr. Snyder reached the end of his active service as president of the University. Despite the fact that the largest part of the Snyder administration had been during war years, when energy was necessarily diverted from purely academic problems to those of the war effort, the operating budget of the University had more than tripled and resources had risen from $54,000,000 to more than $100,000,000. As the Centennial celebration approached, it was clear that the University had achieved maturity and stability.

On October 7, 1949, Dr. Snyder's successor, Dr. James Roscoe Miller, was inaugurated as the twelfth president of Northwestern in an

1949—PRESIDENT J. ROSCOE MILLER addressed guests at inauguration ceremonies in Deering Meadow.

SUMMER'S SPLENDORS and colors covered University grounds. Water and land met at campus border.

1950—SARGENT HALL, named after former Trustee Fred Wesley Sargent, was opened as men's dormitory.

impressive ceremony in Deering Meadow. Dr. Miller, a graduate of Northwestern's Medical School in 1930, had already demonstrated his administrative capabilities as dean of the Medical School between 1941 and 1949. In the new administration Payson S. Wild, Jr. was appointed Vice-President and Dean of Faculties and Jay Gerber Vice-President and Director of Public Relations. Albert C. Van Dusen, associate professor of psychology, became director of the Summer Sessions and special assistant to President Miller in charge of the Centennial celebration.

A number of improvements in the University's facilities, many foreshadowing the forthcoming Centennial, were undertaken or

CONCERT BAND under Glenn Bainum and John Paynter gained respect of all who watched it perform.

completed during President Miller's first year of office. In the autumn of 1949 an annex to Swift Hall, called the Mark W. Cresap Laboratory of Biological Sciences in honor of the eminent trustee, was opened. A new four-story men's dormitory, named in honor of the late Fred Wesley Sargent, prominent Northwestern trustee, was completed in September, 1950. This building, constructed of Lannon stone and brick, is located on the Evanston campus north of the Technological Institute, and has accommodations for 175 men; it contains five dining rooms, a double cafeteria, a lounge and a recreation room.

Asbury Hall, at 1830 Sherman Avenue, built in 1889 as the Norwegian-Danish Methodist Theological Seminary, was purchased in the spring of 1950. The building is used as a dormitory for men of all races and creeds. At the same time Spencer and Holgate houses on University Place were torn down and Alpha Delta Pi sorority house was moved to make way for the future construction of a new women's quadrangle.

The principal goal of the Centennial campaign was announced in October, 1949. A

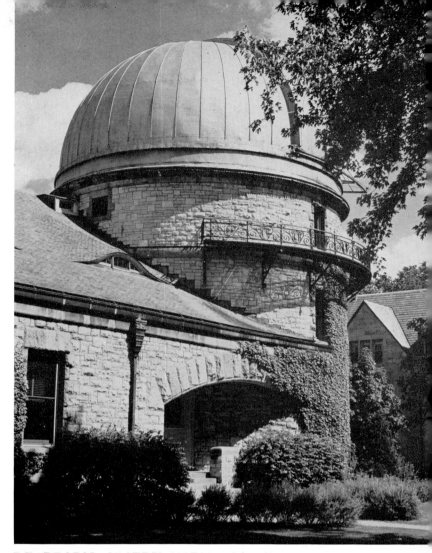

DEARBORN OBSERVATORY with silver dome stood near lake, added fame, beauty to Northwestern.

total of $8,250,000 was to be raised for three new buildings and additional endowment for teaching, research, scholarships, fellowships, and libraries. Most important of the buildings was the three million dollar Centennial Hall, a classroom building for the Evanston campus. A large field house and auditorium, to be named Memorial Hall, was to be built north of Dyche Stadium to provide accommodations for indoor sports events and large gatherings. In addition a classroom building—Evening Study Hall—was to be built on the Chicago Campus to overcome present crowded conditions for evening students. All schools of the University were to be aided by the campaign.

Some additions were made to the curriculum of the College of Liberal Arts. The "freshman year" was expanded with the in-

TELESCOPE IN OBSERVATORY was used not only by faculty and scientists but by student astronomers.

BRAIN WAVE machine installed by psychology department for research was used in study of human behavior.

F. GEORGE SEULBERGER solved problems of innumerable students as University's dean of students.

auguration of a cooperative course based upon experience gained from the B. A. Program, called "Introduction to the Sciences of Human Behavior." The course combined elementary studies in anthropology, psychology, and sociology. Vocational guidance was emphasized by a Career Conference in April, 1950, when leaders in such fields as radio, advertising, teaching, foreign trade, journalism and manufacturing gave lectures and led discussion groups designed to aid students in planning successful careers.

STUDENTS WITH CHAPLAIN James C. McLeod visited court and listened to talk by Judge Julius Miner.

On Sunday, January 29, 1950, the Founders' Day candle-lighting ceremonies were held, with President Miller officiating at the celebration of Northwestern's 99th anniversary. The ceremonies featured the granting of awards to 19 persons by Freedom Foundation Inc. President Emeritus Snyder was given the principal prize of $2,000 and a gold medal for his 1949 Commencement Day address.

In 1948 the Carnegie Corporation of New York made a grant to Northwestern in support of a seminar on African studies. This interdisciplinary seminar has been held in 1948-49 and 1949-50 under the chairmanship of Professor Melville Herskovits. Among the speakers in the seminar were E. E. Sabben-Clare, Cultural Attaché to the British Embassy in Washington; J. S. Harris, Department of Trusteeship, United Nations; Blackwell Smith, sometime president of the Liberia Company, and Uzo Nwagbo of Awka, Nigeria. In the autumn of 1950 plans were laid for holding an Institute on Contemporary Africa at Northwestern during the summer of 1951. Lectures will be held not only in the Institute but also in the various departments of the University so as to reach as wide an audience as possible. Speakers at the Institute will include Vernon McKay, U. S. Delegation, U. N.

STAINED GLASS WINDOW added to beauty of tiny Howes Chapel, where many students have been married.

SCHAFFNER LIBRARY of Commerce, Wieboldt Hall on Chicago Campus, offered good research materials.

MINERALOGICAL BUILDING, first University gymnasium, covered with green ivy during summer months.

1949—MARGERY CARLSON, assistant professor of botany, went plant-hunting in Central America in truck.

VICE-PRESIDENTS Payson S. Wild and J. J. Gerber view booklet of plans for Evanston classroom building.

SPIRE OF SEABURY-WESTERN Theological Seminary rose above trees surrounding sunny campus garden.

Trusteeship Council; Harry Rudin, professor of history, Yale University and Meyer Fortes, professor of anthropology, University of Cambridge. Northwestern has developed a new educational frontier in African affairs, becoming one of the chief centers for this study in the country.

Non-academic activities continued in their variegated pattern. The secretary of the Northwestern Alumni Century Fund, G. Willard King, was appointed executive secretary of the Alumni Association in October, 1949. During the winter of 1949-50 the seventh annual student conference on religion was held under the sponsorship of the Student Religious Council, featuring the theme "Is God a Big Guy on Campus?" Religious leaders from the Chicago area conducted discussion groups and the keynote speaker was Erwin D. Canham, editor of *The Christian Science Monitor*. One of the great future events will be the 1953 general assembly of the World Council of Churches which has accepted the invitation of Dr. Miller and the University (together with Garrett Biblical Institute and Seabury-Western Seminary) to convene in Evanston. It is promised that the assembly will be able to meet in the proposed Memorial Hall.

Other campus events during the year included the Dolphin Club Show "Look Out Below," the WAA-MU Show "Look Who's Talking," the May Week fetes and the celebration of the twenty-fifth anniversary of Orchesis, the University's modern dance society. In the spring of 1950 it was announced that the 27-year-old *Purple Parrot* magazine would be incorporated with *Profile*, which would become the principal student literary publication.

JIGSAW PUZZLE OF LIGHTS patterned Wieboldt Hall, students of Chicago Campus filled evening classes.

The last decade of Northwestern's first century has already shown indications of the lines upon which the University may be expected to develop. The financial prosperity of the University must remain, as ever, largely dependent upon private donations. The experience of the University since 1939 has shown that income from tuition cannot be materially increased without jeopardizing student enrollment. Similarly university investments have, for the present, reached their maximum level of return. It may be possible in the future to obtain government support for specified research projects but there is a danger, demonstrated during the war years, that the University might thus be forced to neglect fundamental research problems in favor of the government-sponsored ones.

Too much government participation in higher education is, in any case, one of the serious dangers with which modern universities are faced. In the words of former President Snyder: "A privately controlled university like Northwestern can make a large contribution to the welfare of society if it is entirely free to choose its own ways of making that contribution. It is conceivable, of course, that education in most of its branches will before long be a pensioner at Washington.

GRADUATE SEMINAR in English met with Professor Virgil Heltzel in Deering Library seminar room.

ALUMNI cut cake at reunion—Mrs. Isabelle Fowler, George Tomlinson, Albert Jones, Mrs. Ruth Wilson.

STUDENT EXTRA-CURRICULAR groups included Chapel Committee, which enjoyed outdoor picnic.

MALCOLM DOLE, chemistry professor, conversed on important international topics with foreign students.

GRADUATION meant handshakes, greetings, diplomas from deans of schools; here Dean Simeon E. Leland.

Should that situation develop, private institutions will probably be forced to join the bread line. But for many reasons we should do all we can to eliminate that possibility."

No new schools have been organized in the past few years and it is probable that the trend, for the near future at least, will be in the direction of strengthening the existing schools and departments within the large and complex framework of the University. Large size

A CAPPELLA CHOIR, in stately black garb, performed several times with Chicago Symphony Orchestra.

FOUNTAIN SQUARE was dedicated on July 4, 1876.   1880's—INDEPENDENCE DAY festivities in square.

CITY HALL, trolleys marked site at turn of century.   1940—SQUARE blended old with modern.

ordinarily means that the relationship between faculty and students is not close, but this tendency has been counteracted by maintenance within the University of the identity and traditions of the various schools and departments. At the same time the intellectual op-

portunities of the entire University have been available to all students.

The Graduate School has steadily raised its standards for advanced degrees since 1939, becoming increasingly selective in admitting first year students. This fundamental prob-

186

lem of selection has received the attention of Dean Arthur Tebbutt for the Graduate School, and of the admissions office of William K. Selden for the University as a whole. The administration of the Graduate School was further strengthened in 1949-50 with the establishment of the office of assistant dean. Larger appropriations for publications, research and fellowships have helped to attract and hold both students and faculty research scholars who seek to advance the frontiers of knowledge.

President Miller and Vice-President Wild showed deep interest in promotion of research, and created a University Faculty Committee on Research to encourage and coordinate investigation and intellectual pioneering among all the faculties. Another phase of the new

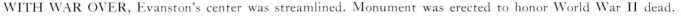

WITH WAR OVER, Evanston's center was streamlined. Monument was erected to honor World War II dead.

GENERAL READING ROOM of library provided comfortable surroundings for general study and research.

organization was the establishment of a central body to direct publication activities— the Committee on Publications.

The University Library, so fundamental to advanced research and the Graduate School itself, was reorganized under the University Librarian, Jens Nyholm. Technical processes were simplified, funds for books, periodicals and salaries were substantially increased and a policy was instituted of cooperating with other Midwestern libraries to reduce unnecessary duplication of purchases and to make easier the interchange of documents and information. In September, 1939 there were 635,795 volumes in the libraries; in 1948 this number had risen to 935,448. The one-millionth volume was presented to the Library in July 1950 by Roger Deering McCormick who had participated in the opening ceremonies for Deering Library eighteen years before.

The year 1949-50 marked the ninetieth anniversary of the School of Medicine. A long-range program of expansion was begun under the leadership of Dean Miller in 1946 and continued under his successor, Dean Richard Young. The establishment of a Department of Nutrition and Metabolism, under the direction of Dr. Tom Spies, and of a Rheumatic Fever Research Institute under Dr. Alvin Coburn were among the first sections of the program. In both cases, the necessary funds came from outside the University, a fortunate circumstance during the trying years of postwar re-establishment. Other parts of the program still to be completed include an Institute of Medical Research, an adjacent 600-bed hospital of the Veterans Administration (build-

ONE MILLIONTH BOOK for Deering Library given in 1950 by Roger McCormick, corner-stone layer of 1932.

GRADUATE RESEARCH FACILITIES in Deering included carrels conveniently near well-supplied stacks.

ing in 1950-51) and several additional hospitals.

The Law School has effected a more logical grouping of required courses and made possible the cooperation of several faculty members in a single course. In these changes Dean Harold Havighurst has presided over an energetic and cooperative faculty. Comments from other law schools indicate that Northwestern has again demonstrated its leadership in legal education.

In 1943 a survey of the School of Dentistry conducted by the Council on Dental Education of the American Dental Association made a number of recommendations, among them closer relationships with hospitals and the employment of more full-time faculty members in the clinical departments. The latter suggestion reflects one of the chronic problems of the School, where a large number of the faculty are successful practitioners as well as teachers and who cannot afford to accept the less remunerative full-time posts which the School can offer. Leadership has been assumed in the fields of research and the graduate training of foreign dentists; research achievements have brought world-wide recognition and this has brought numbers of foreign dentists to Northwestern. It was decided by Dean Charles W. Freeman and the faculty to admit only persons who were already licensed practitioners in their own countries, who could demonstrate their fitness for graduate study and who would return to their homes at the close of their residence at Northwestern; these

men and women now practice throughout the world.

In the past decade the School of Speech has demonstrated a strong appeal to a widespread clientele of undergraduates and, in addition, has made a notable record in research concerning speech and hearing defects. Such research was given strong emphasis by the war and its physical damage to large numbers of men. In many of the diagnostic features of the work the School of Speech and the School of Medicine jointly set new standards in the treatment of auditory and speech injuries.

Between 1939 and 1950 the School of Commerce, the second largest school in the University, expanded its curriculum from an undergraduate program of which the first two years were taken in the College of Liberal Arts and only the last two in the School of Commerce, to a four-year undergraduate program and a full calendar year of graduate work leading to the degree of Master of Business Administration. In 1945 a day division for full-time students was instituted on the Chicago Campus where previously there were only part-time evening students. The evening division, one of the foremost centers of adult education in the Chicago area, found it necessary after the war to limit the number of applicants accepted. One development, greatly desired by the faculty of the School of Commerce, has not been possible because of the shortage of qualified instructors. This is the establishment of more programs of cooperative education with industry, of the type pioneered by

JOB TIME ANALYSIS was demonstrated for Commerce School industrial management class at local plant.

CLASS DAY PROCESSION in Law School Quadrangle gave friends of Northwestern view of academic splendor.

THE "ROCK," between Harris Hall and University Hall, has been social and political center of campus for many years. Originally a fountain, gift of Class of 1902. Plumbing was removed when pipes burst during hard winter.

BOARD OF TRUSTEES, University's governing body, welcomed President Miller to his new office in 1949.

the Technological Institute. In September, 1949, Homer Vanderblue resigned as dean of the School of Commerce for reasons of health and was succeeded by Joseph M. McDaniel, who returned to the University from service with the Economic Cooperation Administration. The graduate division of the School of Commerce was consolidated and moved to the Chicago Campus in the fall of 1950, with Richard Donham in charge as associate dean. The undergraduate division in Evanston was directed by an associate dean, Ernest Davies.

In the School of Education a new program of studies designed to give a general education rather than a narrowly professional one was instituted by Dean James Monroe Hughes in 1945. Graduate work has also been strengthened since 1939, despite the increased demand for teachers with masters' degrees and the temptations in some places to meet the demand in the easiest possible fashion.

Despite the war the School of Journalism had quadrupled its pre-war enrollment by 1946 and with its five-year program had established an outstanding reputation. Its graduates were so much in demand by newspapers, magazines and radio stations that for ten years it has had 100 percent placement of its graduates every year. Carefully selected students came from almost every state and an increasing number of foreign journalists attended for advanced study.

The general curriculum of the School of

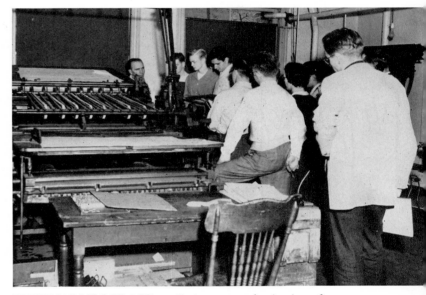

JOURNALISM CLASS studied typographer's plant for understanding of mechanical problems of publication.

NORTHWESTERN REVIEWING STAND had radio panels on such questions as "Are you too old to learn?"

CENTENNIAL COMMITTEE planned celebration of Northwestern's hundred years of development and service.

Music has remained unchanged although its high standards of training have increased the demand for its graduates as teachers of music throughout the country. It early required a four-year course. The University Symphony Orchestra and the A Cappella Choir rank with many professional organizations. The concerts by faculty members and students, presented each year to the public without charge, bring the best music to the North Shore and make the Evanston campus one of the really significant musical centers in the Middle West. Among these programs, presented in 1949-50, were the tenth annual Christmas concert of the combined choral groups, the Easter presentation of Bach's "Mass in B Minor," and the presentation of Brahm's "Requiem Mass," with the Chicago Symphony Orchestra in

TO STUDENTS OF
NORTHWESTERN

OUR UNIVERSITY WAS ESTABLISHED AND IS SUPPORTED BY VOLUNTARY GIVING. ITS FOUNDERS CHOSE THIS WAY TO CONTRIBUTE TO THE SOCIAL PROGRESS OF THEIR TIME. SINCE THEN, THOUSANDS OF ALUMNI AND OTHER FRIENDS HAVE FOLLOWED THEIR GENEROUS EXAMPLE. THESE DONORS ASK NO RETURN SAVE THAT YOU MAKE THE MOST OF THE OPPORTUNITIES THEY HAVE HELPED TO PROVIDE AND THAT YOU, AS FUTURE ALUMNI, CARRY ON THEIR FAITH IN YOUTH AND NORTHWESTERN.

FOUNDERS DAY
JANUARY 28, 1949

THE ALUMNI OF
NORTHWESTERN

BRONZE TABLET in Deering Library, donated by Alumni Association, reminded students of obligation.

STUDENT AFFAIRS were supervised by directorate— Claudine Mason, Roland McGuigan, and Joe Miller.

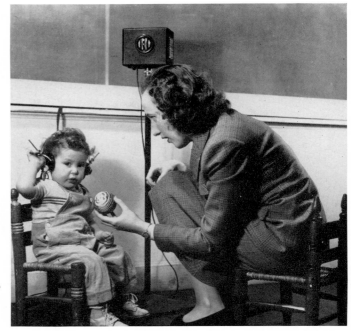

RESEARCH OF SPEECH SCHOOL in speaking and hearing defects has been of service to young and old.

Orchestra Hall. The School of Music has served as a training center for the children of Evanston and it has pioneered the publication of four popular sets of public school music books.

In the summer of 1950 an announcement

LECTURES IN HARRIS HALL attracted students of College of Liberal Arts and those in related fields.

NEW B.A. PROGRAM featured class discussion by faculty and students and helped raise academic standards.

DISCUSSION METHOD aided German class students where correct pronunciation in conversation was stressed.

VISUAL EDUCATION, an educational development made available at Northwestern to augment curriculum.

was made that the School of Music was the recipient of a bequest of over $3,000,000 by the late Mrs. Louis Eckstein. Plans for development made as a result of the announcement included increased salaries for faculty, creation of a number of scholarships, improve-

ment of equipment and increased building accommodations to augment that already in use.

In its eleven years of existence the Technological Institute has rapidly developed its educational functions. In these years more

STUDENTS OF MATHEMATICS relaxed at informal faculty-student tea after heavy quarter schedule of class.

engineering students have completed undergraduate professional sequences in the Institute than in the previous thirty years of engineering education at Northwestern. Since the first class of 97 students was admitted in 1939, 2,616 students, exclusive of V-12 enrollment, have been selected. Moreover, during the war the Institute was responsible for the war instruction of about 20,000 of the persons trained at the University. The war emergency also brought changes in the training program. Academic work was increased by one quarter while cooperative experience was correspondingly reduced from seven to six quarters. Students of the Institute have been active in campus affairs and *The Northwestern Engineer*, a student publication founded in 1941, is one of the best magazines of its type in the country.

Proximity to the metropolitan center of Chicago has made adult education an important element in the curriculum of Northwestern. University College has provided instruction in liberal arts, education and speech in addition to the work of the evening divisions of the schools of Commerce and Journalism. In this phase of academic work students are not so much interested in getting degrees as in fitting themselves to live fuller lives. The need for the future, already discussed in connection with the Centennial campaign, is to provide an adequate building in which this valuable work can better be carried out.

The University has responded in many ways to the call of the community for adult education, to the obvious need in a confused and changing world for the continuity of learning beyond the youthful period when one spends full time within ivy-covered walls. The Northwestern Reviewing Stand has broadcast discussions of current topics over WGN and the Mutual network every Sunday since 1934. Professors are asked to speak before the P.T.A.'s, the League of Women Voters, councils on world affairs, and conferences and meetings innumerable. The local demand was met in a new way in 1950 by the inauguration of a varied series of evening non-credit lecture courses, developed by Dean E. T. McSwain and the University College, and this extension of the classroom and the forum has been well received in both Evanston and Chicago.

It cannot be said that the University enters upon its second century with the future stretching away cloudless to infinity. Economic problems unique in their magnitude and complexity beset the nation, and Northwestern in common with all privately endowed institutions will find it increasingly difficult to perform its functions and make necessary improvements without the vital support of increased endowment. In addition, the threat of war, so dramatically and tragically demonstrated in the summer of 1950, has placed in jeopardy not only Northwestern but the whole purpose of free education and all the ideals of the free world.

Northwestern has weathered every storm of the past; wars, depressions, national and local calamities have hardly done more than delay a development which has gone steadily forward.

But the greatest asset of the University is a tradition of great names. Northwestern was built by men and women who believed strongly in individual initiative, free inquiry and human dignity. They developed this institution to preserve the values of democracy and to offer opportunity to oncoming generations. They preferred to keep their University independent of state control, believing that in this way it could best be a constructive, stimulating influence in state and nation. As builders of Northwestern, they have become a part of the great heritage of America— Evans, Lunt, the Deerings, the Swifts, Patten, Gary, Wilson, Morton, Mayer, Montgomery Ward, Thorne, Abbott, McCormick, Wieboldt, Murphy. . . . Within the halls of the University itself were great teachers, scholars and administrators—Hinman, Noyes, Bonbright, Marcy, Rogers, James, Curme, Holgate, the Blacks, Davis, Wigmore, Cutter, Scott, Snyder. . . . There are also the names of additional thousands—trustees and faculty, staff and students, alumni and other friends—who have given money, service, enthusiasm, and inspiration to the cause of the University. Together they are helping to realize the vision of those nine courageous young men who met one day in May, 1850, to begin a university which built upon an ideal: "Quaecumque sunt vera— Whatsoever things are true."

Pictures Were Obtained from the Following Sources

Acme Photos
Allis-Chalmers Company
Associated Press Photos
Bell and Howell Company
Brandt and Wright, Photographers
Brooks Photos
Capes Photos
Caterpillar Tractor Company
Chicago Architectural Photography Co.
Chicago Daily News
Chicago Historical Society
Chicago Sun-Times
Chicago Tribune
Chicago—Yesterday and Today
Mrs. Caroline Piper Dorr
Evanston Historical Society
Evanston Photographic Service
Evanston Review
Fowler Photographers
Fulton-Lawson Company
Dwight Furness, Photographer
Garrett Biblical Institute
General Electric X-ray Corporation

Hedrich-Blessing Studio
A. Hesler and Son, Photographers
A. Hurter Studios
International Harvester Company
John D. Jones, Photographer
Larry Larimer, Photographer
Patty Ley, Photographer
Northwestern University, An Art Souvenir
Northwestern University in the World War
Official U. S. Coast Guard Photographs
Official U. S. Navy Photographs
Phi Kappa Sigma Fraternity
Picturesque Evanston
Pontiac Photos
E. L. Ray Studio
Alfred Rockefeller, Photographer
C. E. Smith, Photographer
Paul Stone—Raymore
J. D. Toloff Studio
Carl Ullrich, Inc.
R. C. Wieboldt Company
Wide World Photos
Women's Christian Temperance Union

University Sources

Alumni News
Archibald Church Library
Dental School
Industrial Relations Department
Law School
The Neoplasm

Northwestern Engineer
Publicity Office
Sports Publicity Office
Students Publishing Co.
University Archives

The Pictorial History is printed on eighty pound basis Dill and Collins Black and White enamel stock. The body type, number 337 Caslon Monotype, is set twelve point on a fourteen point body. Copy photographs were made by Williams and Meyers, Evanston Photographic Service, and Ken Schmid Studios. Engravings were produced by the Jahn and Ollier Engraving Company, and the printing was done by the Rogers Printing Company of Chicago and Dixon, Illinois. Covers were made by S. K. Smith and Brock and Rankin, both of Chicago. Technical assistance was generously given by Gordon Brightman and Oliver Rogers.

CHICAGO